Recent popular accounts to place the events surrounding the exodus at the Gulf of Aqaba and Saudi Arabia have resulted in creative rewriting of historical and geographical explanations to relocate sites hundreds of miles away from Egypt. Beitzel has gathered all the textual, geographical, and archaeological data that only the discipline of historical geography could produce and provides an exhaustive collection of data to demonstrate that the Red Sea crossing could only have taken place at or near the Gulf of Suez. This is now one of the foundational reference works for any discussion on the geography and context of the exodus event.

—Steven M. Ortiz, Professor of Archaeology and Biblical Studies and Director, Lanier Center for Archaeology, Lipscomb University

Beitzel's study must surely be the definitive word on *yam suf*. No longer can one argue for it referring exclusively to either the Gulf of Suez or the Gulf of Aqaba. His exhaustive list of classical comments on *erythra thalassa* and *mare rubrum* along with his extensive list of dated Trajanic milestones is impressive. One of the most helpful implications of this work is that no one any longer can seriously entertain an Israelite exodus across the Gulf of Aqaba or a Saudi Arabian location for Mt. Sinai.

—Lawrence T. Geraty, President Emeritus, La Sierra University

The core of Beitzel's work, *Where Was the Biblical Red Sea?*, revolves around the question of the location of ancient Israel's deliverance from Egypt. The question that the author sets out to answer: Where is the location of ancient Israel's deliverance from Egypt?

Two recent doctoral dissertations have been published, namely, by Michael D. Oblath (2004) and Glen A. Fritz (2006/2016), in which the question has been shifted foundationally in both time and space. These dissertations focus temporally not on high antiquity but rather on the classical period, i.e., the interlocking civilizations of ancient Greece and Rome. Their authors ask: 1) what did the expression *erythra thalassa* found in the Septuagint (and its Latin equivalent in the Vulgate—*mare rubrum*) actually signify in the biblical texts; 2) what did the same expressions denote in the classical world; and 3) when, chronologically speaking, did these expressions come to be associated with all sectors of today's "Red Sea." Likewise, relative to space, the authors attempt to move the spatial center of the discussion, in this case away from Egypt proper and distinctly onto the Gulf of Aqaba/Elat, hundreds of miles to the east. Related to this is the authors' contention that Mt. Sinai must be sought in the Arabian Peninsula, not in the Sinai Peninsula.

Beitzel posits that there is a pattern of evidence pointing to the location of *yam sûf* and to the Israelite exodus in close proximity to Egypt and not at the Gulf of Aqaba/Elat. He sets forth the pattern of evidence for his position: 1) the meaning of *sûf* and *yam sûf* in the Old Testament and in ancient literature; 2) a "three-day" consideration; and 3) a sequence of Egypt, *yam sûf*, wilderness, Sinai.

Beitzel's paramount purpose in the work is to present primary evidence from both biblical and classical written sources and early cartographically related traditions that fundamentally challenges and ultimately seeks to refute Fritz's two central tenets/hypotheses, namely: 1) "the biblical *Yam Suph* is the Gulf of Aqaba"; and 2) that geographical knowledge of the Gulf of Aqaba/Elat was materially absent throughout the classical period. Continuing in this vein, Beitzel concludes that Fritz's first hypothesis is fundamentally out of step with standard, conventional biblical scholarship. Additionally, Beitzel contends that Fritz's second hypothesis is out of alignment with the discipline of geographical scholarship.

Beitzel contends that an examination of the exodus narratives, as portrayed in the Bible, leads to the firm conclusion that the event occurred in close proximity to Egypt and not at a location hundreds of miles away like the Gulf of Aqaba/Elat.

Beitzel's work has significance for biblical studies. It points out that the exodus is unlikely to have occurred at some place in the Gulf of Aqaba/Elat. In addition, it shows that it is baseless to propose the location of Mt. Sinai in Saudi Arabia.

—Burton MacDonald, Professor Emeritus, Department of
Religious Studies, St. Francis Xavier University

Where did Moses cross the Red Sea? Was it in Egypt or in Arabia? Popular books, some academic ones and TV films maintain he crossed the Gulf of Aqaba into modern Saudi Arabia. Barry Beitzel proves that is wrong! He scrutinizes every piece of information, weighing every argument in great detail to counter misleading and faulty interpretations. No scholar or exegete should overlook the verdict of Beitzel's scholarship: Moses crossed the line of the Suez Canal!"

—Alan R. Millard, Emeritus Rankin Professor of Hebrew &
Ancient Semitic Languages, University of Liverpool

New proposals that challenge long-held traditions often grab headlines, and some may prove true, but the recent contention that the biblical exodus had to be related to the Gulf of Aqaba hundreds of miles from Egypt must now be rejected. With an avalanche of evidence, from a wide variety of sources, Dr. Beitzel demolishes that novel thesis. His comprehensive and compelling argument should put such speculation to rest.

—William L. Kynes, Senior Pastor, Cornerstone
Evangelical Free Church, Annandale, VA

I am surprised by how interested many people remain about the biblical story of Israel's deliverance from Egypt. In my church, located near Fuller Seminary, Caltech University, and the Jet Propulsion Laboratory-NASA, I think this is particularly true. As a pastor, I am asked what the Bible refers to when it speaks about a "Red Sea," whether this event could have happened and, if so, what the location of the exodus might have been. Many who speak to me about these matters are skeptical about the trustworthiness of the scholarship behind some of the popular religious books and films about the subject that are being produced. Because of that, I am thankful for Barry Beitzel's carefully researched *Where Was the Biblical Red Sea?*

Admittedly, much of this work is more technical than most churchgoers will appreciate. However, I find the careful way that Dr. Beitzel makes his case in the body of the work and locates the technical discussions in the notes to be helpful. Those who want to focus on his argument that the Red Sea mentioned in the Bible is located very close to Egypt may do so easily. Those who are concerned about the supporting research for each part of his thesis can also find that with no trouble. Just as important, the meticulous blend of philological data, good biblical exegesis, and scholarly views about the ancient geography of the Nile Delta makes this a very important work for a topic that is central to our faith.

—Greg Waybright, Senior Pastor, Lake Avenue Church, Pasadena, CA

WHERE WAS THE BIBLICAL RED SEA?

Examining the Ancient Evidence

See also these titles from the
Lexham Geographic Commentary Series,
edited by Barry J. Beitzel

Lexham Geographic Commentary on the Gospels

Lexham Geographic Commentary on Acts through Revelation

*Lexham Geographic Commentary on
the Pentateuch (forthcoming)*

*Lexham Geographic Commentary on the
Historical Books (forthcoming)*

*Lexham Geographic Commentary on
Poetry and Prophecy (forthcoming)*

For updates on this series, visit
LexhamPress.com/Geographic-Commentary

WHERE WAS THE BIBLICAL RED SEA?

Examining the Ancient Evidence

Studies in Biblical Archaeology, Geography, and History

BARRY J. BEITZEL

Series Editor: Barry J. Beitzel

LEXHAM PRESS

Where Was the Biblical Red Sea?: Examining the Ancient Evidence
Studies in Biblical Archaeology, Geography, and History

Copyright 2020 Barry J. Beitzel

Lexham Press, 1313 Commercial St., Bellingham, WA 98225
LexhamPress.com

Print ISBN 9781683594383
Digital ISBN 9781683594390
Library of Congress Control Number 2020945363

Series Editor: Barry J. Beitzel
Lexham Editorial: Douglas Mangum, Jessica Parks, James Spinti, Lisa Eary,
Abigail Stocker, Danielle Thevenaz
Cover Design: Kristen Cork
Typesetting: ProjectLuz.com

*This book is affectionately dedicated to my
three children and their spouses—*

Bradley Jay and Heather Colleen Beitzel

Bryan Kent and Dina Lynn Beitzel

Kelly Melinda and Steven Richard Fritz

*—whose loving and thoughtful ways bring immeasurable
gratification and joy to my family*

(Psalm 127:3–5)

CONTENTS

ILLUSTRATIONS

FIGURES

MAPS

TABLES

ABBREVIATIONS

AAAS	*Annales archéologiques arabes Syriennes*
ÄAT	Ägypten und Altes Testament
AB	Anchor (Yale) Bible
ABD	*Anchor Bible Dictionary.* Edited by David Noel Freedman. 6 vols. New York: Doubleday, 1992
ADAJ	*Annual of the Department of Antiquities of Jordan*
ADPV	Abhandlungen des Deutschen Palästina-Vereins
AEL	*Ancient Egyptian Literature: A Book of Readings.* Miriam Lichtheim. 3 vols. Berkeley: University of California Press, 2006
AEO	*Ancient Egyptian Onomastica.* Alan H. Gardiner. 3 vols. London: Oxford University Press, 1947
AHw	*Akkadisches Handwörterbuch.* Wolfram von Soden. 3 vols. Wiesbaden: Harrassowitz, 1965–1981
ANET	*Ancient Near Eastern Texts Relating to the Old Testament.* Edited by James B. Pritchard. 3rd ed. Princeton: Princeton University Press, 1969
ANRW	*Aufstieg und Niedergang der römischen Welt: Geschichte und Kultur Roms im Spiegel der neueren Forschung.* Edited by Hildegard Temporini and Wolfgang Haase. Berlin: de Gruyter, 1972–
Ant.	*Jewish Antiquities.* Josephus
ARCER	American Research Center in Egypt Reports

BA	*Biblical Archaeologist*
BAGRW	*Barrington Atlas of the Greek and Roman World.* Richard J. A. Talbert and Roger S. Bagnall. Princeton: Princeton University Press, 2000
BARIS	BAR International Series
BBRSup	Bulletin for Biblical Research Supplement
BD	Brünnow, R., and A. Domaszewski. *Die Provincia Arabia auf grund zweier in den jahren 1897 und 1898 unternommenen reisen und der berichte früherer reisender.* 3 vols. Strassburg: Trübner, 1904–1909
BDB	Brown, Francis, S. R. Driver, and Charles A. Briggs. *A Hebrew and English Lexicon of the Old Testament.* Oxford: Clarendon, 1906
BN	*Biblische Notizen*
BNP	*Brill's New Pauly: Encyclopaedia of the Ancient World.* Edited by H. Cancik, H. Schneider, and M. Landfester. 22 vols. Leiden: Brill, 2002–2012
c.	circa
CBC	Cambridge Bible Commentary
CC	Continental Commentary
CCSL	Corpus Christianorum: Series Latina
CIL	*Corpus Inscriptionum Latinarum.* Berlin, 1862–
COS	*The Context of Scripture.* Edited by William W. Hallo and K. Lawson Younger Jr. 4 vols. Leiden: Brill, 1997–2016
DCH	*Dictionary of Classical Hebrew.* Edited by David J. A. Clines. 9 vols. Sheffield: Sheffield Phoenix, 1993–2016
DOP	*Dumbarton Oaks Papers*
DOTP	*Dictionary of the Old Testament: Pentateuch.* Edited by T. Desmond Alexander and David W. Baker. Downers Grove, IL: InterVarsity Press, 2003

EHLL	*Encyclopedia of Hebrew Language and Linguistics.* Edited by Geoffrey Khan. 4 vols. Leiden: Brill, 2013
ECC	Eerdmans Critical Commentary
frag(s).	fragment(s)
HACL	History, Archaeology, and Culture of the Levant
HALOT	*The Hebrew and Aramaic Lexicon of the Old Testament.* Ludwig Koehler, Walter Baumgartner, and Johann J. Stamm. Translated and edited under the supervision of Mervyn E. J. Richardson. 2 vols. Leiden: Brill, 2001
IAAR	Israel Antiquities Authority Reports
ICC	International Critical Commentary
IJNA	*International Journal of Nautical Archaeology*
ILS	*Inscriptiones latinae selectae.* Hermann Dessau. 3 vols. Chicago: Ares, 1979.
ISBE	*International Standard Bible Encyclopedia.* Edited by Geoffrey W. Bromiley. 4 vols. Grand Rapids: Eerdmans, 1979–1988
J.	Jebel (Arabic word for mountain)
JAOS	*Journal of the American Oriental Society*
JBL	*Journal of Biblical Literature*
JEA	*Journal of Egyptian Archaeology*
JRASup	Journal of Roman Archaeology Supplement
LÄ	*Lexikon der Ägyptologie.* Edited by Wolfgang Helck, Eberhard Otto, and Wolfhart Westendorf. 7 vols. Wiesbaden: Harrassowitz, 1972
LAE	*The Literature of Ancient Egypt: An Anthology of Stories, Instructions, Stelae, Autobiographies, and Poetry.* Edited by William Kelly Simpson. 3rd ed. New Haven: Yale University Press, 2003
LCL	Loeb Classical Library
LHBOTS	Library of Hebrew Bible/Old Testament Studies
LXX	The Septuagint

MAB	*The New Moody Atlas of the Bible.* Barry J. Beitzel. Chicago: Moody Press, 2009
MP	*millia passuum* (= "1000 paces")
MT	Masoretic Text
N	Nobbe, Carolus Fredericus Augustus. *Claudii Ptolemaei Geographia.* 3 vols. Leipzig: Tauchnitus, 1843–1845
NAC	New American Commentary
NCB	New Century Bible
NICOT	New International Commentary on the Old Testament
NIDOTTE	*New International Dictionary of Old Testament Theology and Exegesis.* Edited by Willem A. VanGemeren. 5 vols. Grand Rapids: Zondervan, 1997
NIVAC	NIV Application Commentary
NK	New Kingdom
OC	*Oriens Christianus: Römische Halbjahrhefte für die Kunde des christlichen Orients*
OTL	Old Testament Library
PAe	*Probleme der Ägyptologie*
pl(s).	plate(s)
PSBA	*Proceedings of the Society of Biblical Archaeology*
RB	*Revue biblique*
RGRW	Religions in the Graeco-Roman World
RITA	*Ramesside Inscriptions Translated and Annotated: Translations.* Kenneth A. Kitchen. 7 vols. Oxford: Blackwell; Chichester: Wiley-Blackwell, 1993–2014
SBLDS	Society of Biblical Literature Dissertation Series
SCS	Septuagint and Cognate Studies
SG	Stückelberger, Alfred, and Gerd Grasshoff. *Klaudios Ptolemaios: Handbuch der Geographie, Griechisch-Deutsch.* 2 volumes. Basel: Schwabe, 2006

SHBC	Smyth & Helwys Bible Commentary
StBibLit	Studies in Biblical Literature (Lang)
T.	Tel/Tell (Hebrew/Arabic word for artificial earthen occupational mound)
TA	*Tel Aviv*
TBA	*Tübinger Bibelatlas.* Edited by Siegfried Mittmann and Götz Schmitt. Stuttgart: Deutsche Bibelgesellschaft, 2001
TDOT	*Theological Dictionary of the Old Testament.* Edited by G. Johannes Botterweck, Helmer Ringgren, and Heinz-Josef Fabry. Translated by John T. Willis et al. 15 vols. Grand Rapids: Eerdmans, 1974–2006
TLG	*Thesaurus Linguae Graecae*
TLL	*Thesaurus Linguae Latinae*
TOTC	Tyndale Old Testament Commentaries
TWOT	*Theological Wordbook of the Old Testament.* Edited by R. Laird Harris, Gleason L. Archer Jr., and Bruce K. Waltke. 2 vols. Chicago: Moody Press, 1980
TynBul	*Tyndale Bulletin*
VNT	*Via Nova Traiana*
VT	*Vetus Testamentum*
W.	Wadi (Arabic word for intermittent stream bed)
WAW	Writings from the Ancient World
WBC	Word Biblical Commentary
WUNT	Wissenschaftliche Untersuchungen zum Neuen Testament
ZDPV	*Zeitschrift des Deutschen Palästina-Vereins*

INTRODUCTION

The question of the location of ancient Israel's deliverance from Egypt has long fascinated and vexed historians, archaeologists, and biblical scholars alike. In addition to several source-critical paradigms or literary analyses, much of the grist for these discussions has naturally arisen from the biblical expressions employed to locate the event (Hebrew: יַם סוּף, *yam sûph* or *yam sûp*, rendered here *yam sûf*; Greek: ἐρυθρὰ θάλασσα, *erythra thalassa*; Latin: *mare rubrum*). Historically speaking, this aspect of the question has tended to revolve around Hebrew philological and lexicographical examination, sometimes including Egyptian lexicography, Old Testament exegesis, and/or an investigation of the ancient geography of the northeastern Nile Delta and its contiguous terrain, especially toward the east.

More recently, however, two doctoral dissertations have been published in which this aspect of the question has been shifted foundationally in both time and space. Thus, for example, these dissertations focus temporally not on high antiquity, at the time of Israel's deliverance from Egypt, but rather on the classical period.[1] They ask what

---

1. My use of "classical" or "classical period" in this study is intended to refer to that general span of cultural history comprised by the interlocking civilizations of ancient Greece and Rome, thus approximating the "Greco-Roman" designation. As such, it is understood in chronological terms to commence with the works of Homer (late eighth century BC) and continue through the decline of the late Roman Empire and the beginning of the Early Middle Ages (ca. AD 600). This is in contradistinction to a particular era of Greek civilization—the "Classical period"—which

1

the expression *erythra thalassa* found in the Septuagint (and its Latin equivalent in the Vulgate—*mare rubrum*) actually signified in the biblical texts, what the same expressions denoted in the classical world, and when chronologically speaking these expressions came to be associated with all sectors of today's Red Sea. Similarly with space, these dissertations attempt to move the spatial center of the discussion, in this case away from Egypt proper and distinctly onto the Gulf of Aqaba/Elat,[2] hundreds of miles to the east (see map 1).

In 2001 Michael D. Oblath earned a PhD in Near Eastern religions from the University of California and the GTU (Berkeley); his dissertation was subsequently published under the title *The Exodus Itinerary Sites: Their Locations from the Perspective of the Biblical Sources.*[3] Glen A. Fritz was awarded a PhD in 2006 in environmental geography from Texas State University, San Marcos; his dissertation was subsequently modified and published, titled *The Lost Sea of the Exodus: A Modern Geographical Analysis.*[4] While Oblath and Fritz differ dramatically in

---

is commonly understood to follow the "Archaic period" and to extend from the end of the last Athenian tyrant (ca. 510 BC) until the death of Alexander the Great (323 BC).

2. Scholars today are well aware of the political overtones implicit in the expressions "Gulf of Aqaba" or "Gulf of Elat." Attempting to avoid the insinuation of modern politics into my discussion, I have typically chosen to employ this admittedly artificial expression.

3. Michael D. Oblath, *The Exodus Itinerary Sites: Their Locations from the Perspective of the Biblical Sources*, StBibLit 55 (New York: Lang, 2004).

4. Glen A. Fritz, "The Lost Sea of the Exodus: A Modern Geographical Analysis" (PhD diss., Texas State University, 2006); Fritz, *The Lost Sea of the Exodus: A Modern Geographical Analysis* (San Antonio, TX: GeoTech, 2016). This book appears to have been privately published by an entity that has only published works by Fritz. To better distinguish the two versions of his work (since they share a title), the year will be included in future citations. In an earlier presentation to an American Schools of Oriental Research audience, I tended to focus more on the work of Oblath, whose views I felt would perhaps hold greater interest in that context. For the same reason, I shall focus my attention here on the work of Fritz. To anyone who may question the motivation or legitimacy of my approach, it is well to bear in mind that this dissertation was completed under the tutelage of a seasoned team of respected professors of geography, within a well-recognized department of geography, and at a long-standing, established university. Moreover, since the geographical aspects of this work are increasingly referenced in popular-level discussions that focus on locating biblical Mt. Sinai inside modern Saudi Arabia, in addition to a growing number of other Christian or Jewish voices which are likewise convinced biblical *yam sûf* must be locationally related to the Gulf of Aqaba/Elat and that Mt. Sinai must be sought in the Arabian Peninsula, not in the Sinai Peninsula, there is a sense in which my critique has more general application (see, e.g., Colin J. Humphreys, *The Miracles*

terms of their dissertation research designs, presuppositions, over-
arching methodologies, use of primary evidence, interaction with
scholarship, historical and geographical interpretation, and conclusions, and while they write from two diverse disciplines, with dissim-
ilar motivations, and probably even with different audiences in mind,
these two scholars nevertheless intersect at one critical juncture in
their presentations. Both authors foundationally anchor their study
of the location of the Israelite exodus on these two central tenets:
(1) all canonical references to *yam sûf* (normally rendered *erythra
thalassa* in the LXX) *must unequivocally and exclusively identify* what
is known today as the Gulf of Aqaba/Elat (Fritz, hypothesis one).[5]
At the same time, both writers insist that (2) all citations of *erythra
thalassa//mare rubrum*[6] in early written secular sources from classical

---

of Exodus: A Scientist's Discovery of the Extraordinary Natural Causes of the Biblical Stories [San
Francisco: Harper, 2003], 263–336; Howard Blum, *The Gold of Exodus: The Discovery of the
True Mount Sinai* [New York: Simon & Schuster, 1998]; Allen Kerkeslager, "Jewish Pilgrimage
and Jewish Identity in Hellenistic and Early Roman Egypt," in *Pilgrimage and Holy Space in Late
Antique Egypt*, ed. David Frankfurter, RGRW 134 [Leiden: Brill, 1998], 208–13; Kerkeslager, "Mt.
Sinai—in Arabia? Ancient Jewish Tradition Locates Holy Mountain," in *Mysteries of the Bible:
From the Location of Eden to the Shroud of Turin; a Collection of Essays Published by the Biblical
Archaeology Society*, ed. Molly Dewsnap Meinhardt [Washington, DC: Biblical Archaeology
Society, 2004], 33–46; Peter Enns, "Exodus Route and Wilderness Itinerary," *DOTP*, 273–77;
Duane A. Garrett, *A Commentary on Exodus*, Kregel Exegetical Library [Grand Rapids: Kregel
Academic, 2014], 104–35, 415–17; Alexander Hool, *Searching for Sinai: The Location of Revelation*
[Nanuet, New York: Feldheim, 2017]).

    5. Fritz, "Lost Sea of Exodus" (2006), 11; Fritz, *Lost Sea of Exodus* (2016), 7.

    6. The equation *erythra thalassa* (or the Attic dialectal variation *erythra thalatta*) = *mare
rubrum* (or *erythraeum mare* or *oceanum rubrum*) is made explicit in a passage from the early
first century BC Latin geographer, Pomponius Mela (*De Chorographia* 3.8.72a). Mela declares:
"the Greeks call *mare rubrum* the '*erythra thalassa*' either because it is that color or because of
Erythras" (an early Persian monarch said to have established his reign over that entire region).
The same equation plainly appears later in the first century, made explicit in a passage from
Pliny the Elder (*Natural History* 6.28.107–9). In the middle of his rather detailed description
of the easternmost world, and how one might sail between Egypt and India, Pliny pauses
parenthetically—and doubtless illustratively—to discuss the 325–324 BC nautical voyage on
the Indian Ocean, between the mouth of the Indus River and the Persian Gulf, undertaken
by Nearchus and Anaxicrates, two of the chief naval commanders of Alexander the Great [cf.
Strabo, *Geography* 2.1.9; 15.2.4; Arrian, *Indica* 20.1–43.14; Arrian, *Anabasis* 6.2.3; 6.19.5; 6.28.6;
7.19.3; 7.20.9; Plutarch, *Alexander* 66.3–4; 73.1]. But then, as he resumes his own story, Pliny
affirms: "at this point [i.e., presumably near the place where Alexander's officers had ended their
investigative oceanic journey] the sea makes a double inroad into the land" [*in hac parte geminum
mare in terras*]. Continuing, the historian from Rome—who had received a naval commission

antiquity *must specifically and invariably exclude* the Gulf of Aqaba/Elat (Fritz, hypothesis two).[7] Accordingly, both Oblath and Fritz hold that classical references to the Red Sea (*erythra thalassa*) and biblical references to the exodus event found in the LXX (*erythra thalassa*) must absolutely and consistently identify mutually exclusive bodies of water.

While Oblath and Fritz have their own individual and separate reasons for advancing their central underlying tenets, it is clear that in both cases these notions play a quintessential role in their respective understanding and interpretation of the exodus event. Moreover, both scholars argue the certainty and invariability of their two foundational assertions on absolute grounds. There are no exceptions—neither in biblical literature nor in classical literature. For them, biblical *yam sûf* corresponds *solely* with the Gulf of Aqaba/Elat (to them, mistakenly rendered *erythra thalassa* in the LXX and *mare rubrum* in the Vulgate), but in their view the Gulf of Aqaba/Elat is *never* so designated by the use of *erythra thalassa//mare rubrum* in secular classical sources.

The nature or the exact location of the exodus event, however conceptualized, lies beyond the immediate purview of this study.[8] Rather, my paramount purpose here is to present primary evidence from both biblical and classical written sources and early

---

himself during the reign of the emperor Vespasian—summarizes the nomenclature of this sea as follows: "the name given to the (entire) sea by our countrymen is '*Rubrum*,' while the Greeks call it '*Erythrum*' [*quod Rubrum dixere nostri, Graeci Erythrum … aut*]." Then, as if to clarify for his readers the full extent of the body of water he has in mind, Pliny formally identifies the "double inroad" or succession of bays in this way: "the gulf on the east is called '*Persicus*' [i.e., the Persian Gulf]" (*sinus … is qui ab oriente est Persicus appellatur*) and "on the other side [of Arabia] is a second bay known as '*sinu Arabico*' [i.e., the Arabian Gulf/Red Sea]" (*rursus altero ambitur sinu Arabico nominato*). Later, this same equation unambiguously appears in the work of Jerome, both in his translation of Eusebius's *Onomasticon*, where the phrase *erythra thalassa* is consistently rendered with the Latin expression *mare rubrum* (see R. Steven Notley and Ze'ev Safrai, *Eusebius, Onomasticon: The Place Names of Divine Scripture* [Leiden: Brill, 2005], §901/164.7–10), and also in his translation of the Vulgate (see table 1 below).

7. Fritz, "Lost Sea of Exodus" (2006), 12; Fritz, *Lost Sea of Exodus* (2016), 7.

8. Consult most recently in this regard Thomas E. Levy, Thomas Schneider, and William H. C. Propp, eds., *Israel's Exodus in Transdisciplinary Perspective: Text, Archaeology, Culture, and Geoscience* (New York: Springer, 2015); James K. Hoffmeier, Alan R. Millard, and Gary A. Rendsburg, eds., *"Did I Not Bring Israel Out of Egypt?" Biblical, Archaeological, and Egyptological Perspectives on the Exodus Narratives*, BBRSup 13 (Winona Lake, IN: Eisenbrauns, 2016).

cartographically related traditions that fundamentally challenges and ultimately seeks to refute these two central tenets (and, as a consequence, to confront the seminally significant biblical implications that derive from them). As a preliminary response, I will contend that the weight and preponderance of both historic and contemporary biblical scholarship and exegesis make Fritz's hypothesis one idiosyncratic and highly doubtful, and that the evidentiary written record from the classical period renders his hypothesis two baseless and indefensible.[9] As I hope to demonstrate, his work represents a series of assertions that must stand almost entirely without the benefit of objective evidentiary support from antiquity. It seems fitting to declare that Fritz's hypothesis one is considerably out of alignment with established scholarship in the discipline of biblical studies, just as the essence of his hypothesis two stands far beyond the range of conventional scholarship in the discipline of geographical studies.

SUMMARY OF KEY CONCLUSIONS

- When the Hebrew Bible references *yam sûf* ("Sea of Reeds/Papyrus," or "Re(e)d Sea"; translated "Red Sea" in most English versions), several different bodies of water may in context be in view, including the modern Gulf of

---

9. Even beyond the evidence presented here, and in addition to what might be considered the decided scholarly consensus of needing to interpret the biblical expressions *yam sûf* and *erythra thalassa* geographically within their individual contexts, rather than assigning them a static and unequivocal meaning throughout the canon (refer to table 1), this means that Fritz must also shoulder the heavy burden of demonstrating that the Jewish translators of the LXX, presumably at Ptolemaic invitation and sponsorship—while doing their work at the very moment when geographical knowledge of all segments of the classical Red Sea was expanding exponentially as the result of extensive nautical exploration undertaken by Alexander the Great and the early Ptolemaic kings of Egypt, and while translating in Alexandria, the very city where this newfound, first-hand accumulated knowledge was being documented, disseminated, and employed for both scientific and imperial purposes—adopted for their translation of *yam sûf* the well-known and commonly attested classical expression *erythra thalassa*, but yet, at the same time (according to Fritz) these translators created and rigidly applied a stunningly original geographical definition of *erythra thalassa* that was uniquely at variance with Alexandrian scholarship and normative classical usage.

Suez, the Gulf of Aqaba/Elat, or an inland lake separating Egypt from Sinai.[10]

- When classical literature references the "Red Sea" (Greek: *erythra thalassa*; Latin: *mare rubrum*), several different bodies of water may be in view, including the Bay of Bengal, the Indian Ocean, the Persian Gulf, the Gulf of Aden, the classical Gulf of Arabia (= modern Red Sea), the Gulf of Suez, or the Gulf of Aqaba/Elat.

- When rendering *yam sûf* with Greek *erythra thalassa*, the third century BC Jewish scholars who translated the Hebrew Bible into Greek (i.e., the Septuagint = LXX) follow a well-established, standard classical practice, according to which a variety of different bodies of water may be referenced by use of the expression.

- An examination of the exodus narratives as portrayed in the Bible leads to the firm conclusion that the event occurred in close proximity to Egypt and not at a location hundreds of miles away.

- A number of significant achievements in the exact sciences during the classical period, including within the disciplines of geography and cartography, were subsequently lost to the world for a time, ironically in large part as the result of the emergence of Christianity as a dominant force, followed by the decline of the Roman Empire and the dim arrival of the Early Middle Ages.

---

10. Key Old Testament texts for this study include Exod 2:1–10; 12:37–42; 13:17–22; 14:1–31; 15:22–27; Num 20:14–21:26; 33:1–49; Deut 1:1, 1:19–2:15.

Chapter 1

EVIDENCE FROM BIBLICAL SOURCES

I n this chapter, I survey biblical sources relating to the phrase *yam sûf*. These sources variously locate *yam sûf* at the Gulf of Aqaba/ Elat as well as in close proximity to Egypt. The biblical expression is not applied only to one specific location.

I begin with an assessment of Fritz's hypothesis one: "The biblical *Yam Suph* is the Gulf of Aqaba."[1] In an effort to undergird this central hypothesis, Fritz argues that of the twenty-four canonical citations of Hebrew *yam sûf*, seven of these texts *mandate* the Gulf of Aqaba/Elat as the referent (Exod 23:31; Num 14:25; 21:4; Deut 1:40; 2:1; 1 Kgs 9:26; Jer 49:21; see table 1 below). At this point Fritz is adhering to a fairly standard scholarly assessment (see below). So far, so good, though I hasten to add that none of these seven texts relates directly or indirectly to the location where Israel experienced its deliverance from Egypt. Instead, these narratives point (1) to a setting of boundaries for Israel's eventual possession of its land (Exod 23); (2) to a location encountered by Israel during its sojourn, after rejecting the report of the twelve spies, spending considerable time in and around

---

1. Fritz "Lost Sea of Exodus" (2006), 12, 174–75; Fritz, *Lost Sea of Exodus* (2016), 7, 84–86.

Kadesh-barnea, and then attempting to bypass the land of Edom en route to the promised land (Num 14, 21; Deut 1, 2); (3) to Solomon's naval venture to the land of Ophir (1 Kgs 9); or (4) to a place where cries of disaster could be heard, resulting from destruction inflicted upon the land of Edom (Jer 49). None of these seven texts manifests a context of Israel's deliverance from Egypt and in particular at the water of *yam sûf.*

But a critical issue arises with this hypothesis when it is subsequently converted from these seven texts into an absolute and inviolable dogma and is required to be interpreted in this way in *all* canonical citations. In this regard, Fritz asserts: "biblical *Yam Suph* corresponds *solely* with the Gulf of Aqaba,"[2] or he states, "This hypothesis, based strictly on the biblical record, must harmonize with the *entire* biblical account of *Yam Suph* or it will be falsified."[3]

It is curiously revealing that, at this point in his discussion, Fritz makes almost no reference to authoritative biblical scholarship—neither in commentary form nor in reference literature—because, in point of fact, his unsupported assertion stands in diametric opposition to a vast array of established, conventional scholarship across a very wide theological spectrum. It is as if Fritz has turned a blind eye to these rich biblical and exegetical scholarly traditions. Credible research almost always involves a process of engagement with scholars and knowledge past and present, especially when one is attempting to stake out new ground and is arguing at variance with established scholarship. But here this element is largely absent. Fritz's argumentation at this point strikes me as a case of what the widely recognized authority of logic, David Hackett Fischer, identifies as "the fallacy of the presumptive proof," which "consists in advancing a proposition and then shifting the burden of proof or disproof to others."[4]

---

2. Fritz, "Lost Sea of Exodus" (2006), 11 (emphasis added).

3. Fritz, *Lost Sea of Exodus* (2016), 7 (emphasis added).

4. David Hackett Fischer, *Historical Fallacies: Toward a Logic of Historical Thought* (New York: HarperPerennial, 1970), 48–49.

In conformity with the usage of *erythra thalassa* in classical literature (see table 3 below), translators of the LXX appear to employ the
expression with flexible elasticity and variability. Thus, for example,
the Gulf of Aqaba/Elat can well be in view (e.g., Num 21:4; Deut
1:40; 2:1). In context, these texts describe a delegation of Israelite
messengers who had been dispatched from Kadesh-barnea to the
king of Edom and who had unsuccessfully requested that the king
might permit Israel safe passage through his land as far as the King's
Highway, to the east. The king's denial thus necessitated that Israel was
obliged to undertake an indirect, circuitous journey around the land
of Edom to accomplish its mission. In the account of Numbers (21:4),
the Israelites "departed" (√*nsʿ*) from the vicinity of Kadesh-barnea
and Mt. Hor, both of which are located in the southern extremity of
Judah and in close proximity to Naḥal Zin.[5] They are said to have
traveled on the "road to the Red Sea" (*derek yam-sûf*, rendered *hodos
epi thalassan erythran* in the LXX) that would enable them to circum-
vent the land of Edom. Similarly, in Deuteronomy (1:40; 2:1), Israel
"turned" (√*pnh*) away from Canaan (see Num 14:25) and "departed"
(√*nsʿ*) from Kadesh-barnea on the "road to the Red Sea" (*derek yam-
sûf*, rendered *hodos thalassa erythra* in LXX). This text then speaks of
their moving beyond the "Arabah road" (*midderek hāʿărābâ*; cf. Deut
2:8a) and the sites of Elath and Ezion-geber and "turning northward"
(*pənû lākem ṣāpônāh*; cf. 2:3), presumably "taking a roadway in the
direction of the wilderness of Moab" (*wannēpen wannaʿăbōr derek
midbar môʾāb*; cf. 2:8b), on a journey that would enable them to skirt
Mt. Seir (cf. Judg 11:18).[6]

Admittedly, the geography entailed in Israel's recorded itinerary
from Kadesh, around Edom and Mt. Seir, as far as Abel-shittim on the
Plains of Moab, is surely freighted with other sorts of extremely vexed

---

5. Consult, e.g., Denis Baly, *The Geography of the Bible*, 2nd ed. (New York: Harper & Row,
1974), 247–51; Anson F. Rainey and R. Steven Notley, *The Sacred Bridge* (Jerusalem: Carta,
2006), 35, 121; *MAB*, 110–11.

6. See, e.g., Yohanan Aharoni, *The Land of the Bible: A Historical Geography* (Philadelphia:
Westminster, 1979), 203 (map 14).

and complicated textual and text-critical questions,[7] but in no written scenario of which I am aware do the Israelites physically backtrack in a southwesterly direction from Kadesh-barnea and (re)visit the Gulf of Suez while attempting to bypass Edom/Mt. Seir. Therefore *yam sûf* (rendered *thalassa erythrē* in the LXX) in these texts must denote another body of water, and with rather compelling textual and geographical logic, scholars from across the theological spectrum hold this designation to be the Gulf of Aqaba/Elat (see map 1).[8]

On the other hand, LXX translators employ *erythra thalassa* in a cluster of texts where the referent is not the Gulf of Aqaba/Elat and seems clearly to be either the Gulf of Suez or a contiguous or nearly contiguous inland lake along the isthmus of Suez between the Mediterranean Sea and the Gulf of Suez (see table 1 below). The account is describing the location of an Israelite wilderness encampment between Marah/Elim and the wilderness of Sin, en route to Mt. Sinai. According to the Exodus narrative (Exod 15:22–27), after being

---

7. See, e.g., the recent discussions of Thomas B. Dozeman, "Biblical Geography and Critical Spatial Studies," in *Constructions in Space I: Theory, Geography, and Narrative*, ed. Jon L. Berquist and Claudia V. Camp, LHBOTS 481 (London: T&T Clark, 2007), 87–108; Dozeman, *Commentary on Exodus* (Grand Rapids: Eerdmans, 2009); Angela R. Roskop, *The Wilderness Itineraries: Genre, Geography, and the Growth of Torah*, HACL 3 (Winona Lake, IN: Eisenbrauns, 2011), 139–43, 186, 194–95.

8. Roskop, *Wilderness Itineraries*, 196–98, 277; Lloyd R. Bailey, *Leviticus–Numbers*, SHBC 3 (Macon, GA: Smyth & Helwys, 2005), 444–47; Baruch A. Levine, *Numbers 1–20: A New Translation with Introduction and Commentary*, AB 4 (New York: Doubleday, 1993), 368–69; Duane L. Christensen, *Deuteronomy 1:1–21:9*, WBC (Nashville: Nelson, 2001), 33–34; R. Dennis Cole, *Numbers*, NAC 3B (Nashville: Broadman & Holman, 2000), 346; John William Wevers, *Notes on the Greek Text of Numbers*, SCS 46 (Atlanta: Scholars Press, 1998), 340; Eugene H. Merrill, *Deuteronomy*, NAC 4 (Nashville: Broadman & Holman, 1994), 84, 90–92; R. K. Harrison, *Numbers: An Exegetical Commentary* (Grand Rapids: Baker, 1992), 275; Moshe Weinfeld, *Deuteronomy 1–11: A New Translation with Introduction and Commentary*, AB 5 (New York: Doubleday, 1991), 158–61; Jacob Milgrom, *Numbers: The Traditional Hebrew Text with the New JPS Translation*, JPS Torah Commentary (Philadelphia: Jewish Publication Society, 1990), 113, 173; A. D. H. Mayes, *Deuteronomy*, NCB (Grand Rapids: Eerdmans, 1981), 132–36; Gordon J. Wenham, *Numbers*, TOTC (Downers Grove, IL: InterVarsity Press, 1981), 156–57; Peter C. Craigie, *The Book of Deuteronomy*, NICOT (Grand Rapids: Eerdmans, 1976), 105–7; John Gray, *A Critical and Exegetical Commentary on Numbers*, ICC (Edinburgh: T&T Clark, 1976), 160, 277, 443; Martin Noth, *Numbers: A Commentary*, OTL (London: SCM, 1968), 110; S. R. Driver, *A Critical and Exegetical Commentary on Deuteronomy*, 3rd ed., ICC (Edinburgh: T&T Clark, 1965), 34; Alois Musil, *The Northern Ḥeğāz: A Topographical Itinerary*, Oriental Explorations and Studies 1 (New York: AMS Press, 1926), 264.

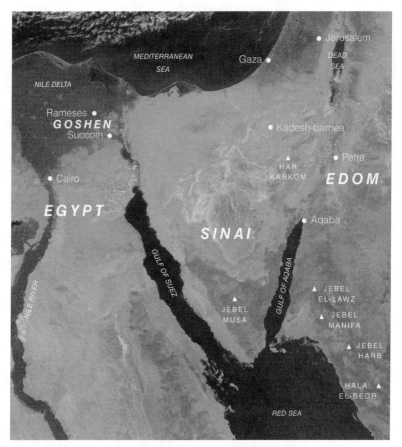

MAP 1: **Satellite view of the Nile Delta and the Sinai Peninsula**

Labelled satellite image displaying terrain between the Nile Delta and mountains to the east of the Gulf of Aqaba/Elat

delivered at *yam sûf* (rendered *thalassēs erythras* in the LXX), Israel traveled three days (*šəlōšet yāmîm*) in the wilderness of Shur (*mid-bar-šûr*; cf. Gen 16:7, *bammidbār ʿal-hāʿayin bəderek šûr*) and arrived at the site of Marah (LXX, *Pikria* ["bitter"]), followed immediately by arriving at Elim (LXX, *Ailim*), where there were twelve springs of water and seventy palm trees. In the essentially synoptic if somewhat

amplified record of Numbers (33:8–9), after passing through the
midst of the sea (*bətôk hayyām;* rendered *meson tēs thalassēs*), Israel
traveled three days (*šəlōšet yāmîm*) in the wilderness of Etham (*midbar
ʾētām*) and again is said to have arrived at Marah (LXX, *Pikria*), once
again followed immediately by the site of Elim (LXX, *Ailim*), with its
twelve springs and seventy palm trees.

It is unclear whether the wilderness of Shur and the wilderness
of Etham are being differentiated or equated in these texts (cf. LXX
Num 33:8, "into the wilderness"). Both geographical entities must
be sought in western Sinai and in close proximity to Egypt's eastern
border (see discussion below in §§2.3 and 2.4), but the exact location
or perimeter of the terrain involved cannot be established with absolute certainty. Whatever the case, both of these texts demand that the
road station of Marah be sought a distance of approximately three
days' journey from the point of the exodus event and only a few additional days' travel from the delta sites of Rameses (Khatana/Qantir;
cf. Exod 12:37; Num 33:5a) and Succoth (Tell el-Maskhuta; cf. Exod
13:20; Num 33:5b).[9] Accordingly, and assuming the named sites to
be reflecting actual historical locations along an itinerary route, these
texts with the greatest probability are pointing toward the Gulf of Suez
or a lake located nearby, a view once again embraced by numerous
biblical scholars from across a wide theological spread within the
discipline (see map 2).[10]

---

9. An abundance of literature is available on this front, on which refer to William G. Dever,
"Is There Any Archaeological Evidence for the Exodus?" in *Exodus: The Egyptian Evidence*,
ed. Ernest S. Frerichs and Leonard H. Lesko (Winona Lake, IN: Eisenbrauns, 1997), 70–71;
Jacobus Van Dijk, "The Amarna Period and the Later New Kingdom (c. 1352–1069 BC)," in
The Oxford History of Ancient Egypt, ed. Ian Shaw (New York: Oxford University Press, 2003),
286–303; John S. Holladay, *Cities of the Delta, Part III: Tell el-Maskhuta: Preliminary Report on
the Wadi Tumilat Project 1978–1979*, ARCER 6 (Malibu, CA: Undena, 1982), 3–9; Jo Ann H.
Seely, "Succoth," ABD 6:217; Roskop, *Wilderness Itineraries*, 196.

10. Cf., e.g., Roskop, *Wilderness Itineraries*, 250; Dozeman, *Exodus*, 306–9; William H.
C. Propp, *Exodus 19–40: A New Translation with Introduction and Commentary*, AB 2A (New
York: Doubleday, 2006), 749–55; Cole, *Numbers*, 521; Baruch A. Levine, *Numbers 21–36: A New
Translation with Introduction and Commentary*, AB 4A (New York: Doubleday, 2000), 517–18;
Harrison, *Numbers*, 403–5; Nahum M. Sarna, *Exodus: The Traditional Hebrew Text with the
New JPS Translation*, JPS Torah Commentary (Philadelphia: Jewish Publication Society), 84;

Beyond this array of commentary and monographic sources, standard reference tools in the field—again, apparently substantially ignored by Fritz—likewise consistently construe biblical *yam sûf* in context to be referencing either (1) the Gulf of Aqaba/Elat; (2) the Gulf of Suez; or (3) one or another of the inland lakes separating Egypt from Sinai.[11] In a rather nonengaging, dismissive manner, and

Milgrom, *Numbers*, 276; Philip J. Budd, *Numbers*, WBC 5 (Waco, TX: Word, 1984); Wenham, *Numbers*, 225–26; W. Gunther Plaut, *The Torah, A Modern Commentary: Numbers* (New York: Union of American Hebrew Congregations, 1979), 318; Gray, *Numbers*, 443; Brevard S. Childs, *The Book of Exodus: A Critical, Theological Commentary*, OTL (Philadelphia: Westminster, 1974), 229–30, 265; R. E. Clements, *Exodus*, CBC (Cambridge: Cambridge University Press, 1972), 81–82, 96; Umberto Cassuto, *A Commentary on the Book of Exodus* (Jerusalem: Magnes, 1983), 183; J. J. Simons, *The Geographical and Topographical Texts of the Old Testament* (Leiden: Brill, 1959), 251–52; Martin Noth, "Der Schauplatz des Meereswunders," in *Festschrift Otto Eissfeldt zum 60. Geburtstage 1. September 1947: Dargebracht von Freunden und Verehrern*, ed. Johann Fück (Halle: Max Niemeyer, 1947), 186, 189.

11. See *NIDOTTE* 3:943; *TWOT* 2:620; *TDOT* 10:193–96; BDB, 693; HALOT, 414, 747; *DCH* 6:134. It is fairly common for a given biblical toponym to be used to designate more than one location, particularly when the name is composed of a common geographical or a divine element (e.g., Bethlehem; Beth-shemesh; Beth-horon; Gibeah; Migda/ol; Gilgal; Ram[ah]; Carmel; Succoth; Hammath; Rimmon, Janoah; Abel/Abila; Socoh; Timnah; Ataroth; Hazor; Jarmuth; Emmaus; Gadara; Philadelphia). There appear to be as many as six different locations named Kadesh/Kedesh ("sanctuary/holy place"), five locations named Mizpah ("watch-tower"), and four locations named Aphek ("fortress").

Another significant aspect of this discussion in which Fritz seems almost oblivious to the Hebrew text and to authoritative contemporary scholarship has to do with the semantics of the Hebrew word *yām* ("sea") itself. Relying in this regard largely on James Strong (*Strong's Exhaustive Concordance*), Fritz argues, without the use of additional evidentiary support, that the word must designate an "ocean" or a "true sea" and was never used to denote the Gulf of Arabia, the Gulf of Suez, or any of the smaller swamp-like inland lakes between the Mediterranean Sea and the Gulf of Suez. See Fritz, "Lost Sea of Exodus" (2006), 194–97; Fritz, *Lost Sea of Exodus* (2016), 98–99, 172–85. A glance at a number of standard lexical/semantic authorities (e.g., BDB, 411; HALOT, 413–14; *NIDOTTE* 2:463; *TDOT* 6:91; *TWOT* 1:381; *DCH* 4:223) suggests otherwise. With good reason, these sources isolate and identify at least four discrete semantic fields for *yām*: (1) *a true sea*, e.g., (a) the Mediterranean Sea (e.g., Num 13:29; Josh 5:1; Jonah 1:4; also called the "great sea" in Josh 15:12; Ezek 47:10; "western sea" in Deut 11:24; Joel 2:20; "sea of the Philistines" in Exod 23:31); (b) the Red Sea (e.g., Exod 15:4; Num 21:4; 33:8–11; Deut 1:40; also called the "sea of Egypt" in Isa 11:15); and possibly (c) the Persian Gulf (e.g., Isa 21:1 [1QIsᵃ reads "word of the sea" (*dbr* vs. *mdbr*); omitted in LXXᴮ; for the Akkadian expression—*māt tâmti* ("land of the sea")—plausibly applied to the region near the Persian Gulf, see CAD 18, s.v. "tâmtu," esp. pp. 154–56]); (2) *an inland lake*, e.g., (a) the Sea of Galilee/ Kinnereth (e.g., Num 34:11; Deut 3:17; Josh 12:3; 13:27; cf. Barry J. Beitzel, "The *Via Maris* in Literary and Cartographic Sources," BA 54.2 [1991]: 66–67); or (b) the Dead/Salt Sea (e.g., Gen 14:3; Num 34:3; Deut 3:17; 4:49; Josh 3:16; 18:19; 2 Kgs 14:25; Jer 48:32 [possibly read "sea of Jazer" in MT]; Joel 2:20); (3) *a large river*, e.g., (a) the Euphrates River (e.g., Jer 51:36); or (b) the Nile River (e.g., Isa 19:5 [see *yᵊʾôrê māẓôr* in 19:6 and *yᵊʾōr* three times in 19:7]; 27:1;

without advancing corroborating evidence of any sort, Fritz incredulously regards this as equivocal thinking, "symptomatic of the confusion" that traditional scenarios create.[12]

Table 1 below brings together all Old Testament references to the *yam sûf*, illustrating the way those references are rendered in the LXX and Vulgate and indicating the likely body of water in view in each case.

TABLE 1: Textual correlation of *yam sûf, erythra thalassa,* and *mare rubrum*

Textual citation	MT	LXX	Vulgate	Probable referent
Following MT versification	x = *yam sûf*	x = *erythra thalassa*[13]	x = *mare rubrum*[14] * = 1590 Latin Bible	POE = crossing-point of the exodus event
(1) Exod 10:19[15]	x [with *h-*]	x	x*	Gulf of Suez

Ezek 32:2; Nah 3:8); and (4) *a large bronze cultic basin found in the temple courtyard* (e.g., 1 Kgs 7:23–44; 2 Chr 4:2–15; Jer 27:19; 52:20). In addition, *yām* can be employed rather generically for water per se (cf. Gen 1:26; 22:17; Exod 20:11; Josh 15:5).

12. Fritz, *Lost Sea of Exodus* (2016), 103.

13. These Greek words may occur in an inverted sequence and/or in capitalized or uncapitalized form; case endings occur as a function of syntax, and accents normally appear in the context of case endings and at times syntax.

14. These Latin words may occur in an inverted sequence and/or in capitalized or uncapitalized form. As with Greek, Latin case endings occur as a function of syntax.

15. Whether viewed through the lens of proposed Hebrew sources related to canonical compositionalism, or through the more conventional lens of essential Mosaic authorship, the number and distribution of canonical citations make clear the fact that various biblical authors and translators consistently understood the expressions *yam sûf, erythra thalassa,* and *mare rubrum* in a variety of ways. This is entirely consistent with the common practice of classical writers. Thus, e.g., for Greek *erythra thalassa,* see Herodotus (2.158, he identifies the Gulf of Suez isthmus; 4.37, Arabian Sea; 6.20, Persian Gulf); Eusebius (*Onomasticon* 6/6:17, Gulf of Aqaba; 655/124:25, Gulf of Suez isthmus; 901/164:7, Persian Gulf); Josephus (*Ant.* 1.39, Persian Gulf; 1.239, Gulf of Arabia; 2.315, Gulf of Suez isthmus; 8.163, Gulf of Aqaba/Elat); Diodorus (1.19.6, Indian Ocean; 1.33.8–12, Gulf of Suez; 19.100.5–6, Persian Gulf). For a few examples of the fluid use of Latin *mare rubrum,* see Quintus Curtius (*History of Alexander* 4.7.18, referencing the modern Red Sea; 5.1.15, Persian Gulf; 8.9.6, Bay of Bengal); Pliny the Elder (*Natural History* 6.35.196, Gulf of Arabia; 16.80.22, Persian Gulf); Jerome (his translation of Eusebius). In a few

Textual citation	MT	LXX	Vulgate	Probable referent
(2) Exod 13:18	x	x	x*	POE
(3) Exod 15:4	x [plus b-]	x	x*	POE
(4) Exod 15:22	x [plus min]	x	x*	Gulf of Suez or POE!
(5) Exod 23:31	x [plus min]	x	x*	Gulf of Aqaba/ Elat
(6) Num 14:25	x	x	x*	Gulf of Aqaba/ Elat
(7) Num 21:4	x	x	x*	Gulf of Aqaba/ Elat!
(8) Num 33:10	x	x	x*	Gulf of Suez!
(9) Num 33:11	x [plus min]	x	x* [33:10b]	Gulf of Suez!
(10) Deut 1:1	sûf	x [ᴮ text][16]	x	Uncertain
(11) Deut 1:40	x	x	x*	Gulf of Aqaba/ Elat!
(12) Deut 2:1	x	x	x*	Gulf of Aqaba/ Elat!
(13) Deut 11:4	x	x[17]	x*	POE
(14) Josh 2:10	x	x	x*	POE
(15) Josh 4:23	x [plus l-]	x	x* [4:24]	POE
(16) Josh 24:6a	sûf [with h-]	x[18]	mare [so 1590 Latin Bible]	POE
(17) Josh 24:6b	x	x[19]	x*	POE
(18) Judg 11:16	x	x [ᴬ text][20]	x* [11:18]	Uncertain

instances, a classical author seems to equivocate inside one and the same context (e.g., Arrian, *Indica* 43.1.1, *Erythra thalassa* references the Persian Gulf, but 43.1.6, Indian Ocean).

16. LXXᴬ reads *erythra*. Though they ultimately have an uncertain referent, the texts of Deut 1:1 and Judg 11:16 have been included on table 1, leading to a total of twenty-six entries.

17. The citation contains an intermediate *tēs*.

18. The citation contain an intermediate *tēn*.

19. The citation contain an intermediate *tēn*.

20. LXXᴮ reads *thalassa siph*.

Textual citation	MT	LXX	Vulgate	Probable referent
(19) 1 Kgs 9:26²¹	x	eschatē thalassa²² [= 3 Kgdms 9:26]	x* [= 3 Kgdms 9:26]	Gulf of Aqaba/Elat!
(20) Neh 9:9	x	x	x* [= 2 Esdras 9:9]	POE
(21) Ps 106:7	x [plus b-]	x [= 105:7]	x²³ [= 105:7]	POE
(22) Ps 106:9	x [plus b-]	x [= 105:9]	x* [= 105:9]	POE
(23) Ps 106:22	x	x [= 105:22]	x* [= 105:22]	POE
(24) Ps 136:13	x	x [= 135:13]	x* [= 135:13]	POE
(25) Ps 136:15	x [plus b-]	x [= 135:15]	x* [= 135:15]	POE
(26) Jer 49:21	x [plus b-]	thalassa²⁴	x*	Gulf of Aqaba/Elat

21. The 2 Chr 8:17 synoptic text reads ʿal-śĕpat hayyām, and the LXX reads parathalassios.

22. The expression eschatē thalassa also appears in LXX Deut 34:2 (for hayyām hāʾaḥărôn); Josh 1:4 (for hayyām haggādôl); and Zech 14:8 (for hayyām hāʾaḥărôn), where it unambiguously denotes the Mediterranean Sea.

23. The 1590 Latin Bible reads mare.

24. The LXXᴬ citation is found in Jer 30:15; LXXᴮ occurs in Jer 29:21.

Chapter 2

EVIDENCE FOR THE *YAM SÛF* IN CLOSE PROXIMITY TO EGYPT

A pattern of evidence points to the location of the *yam sûf* and the related events described in the story of the Israelite exodus being in close proximity to Egypt, and *not* in the vicinity of the Gulf of Aqaba/Elat, which is separated from Rameses and Egypt by more than two hundred land miles (330 km).

2.1 THE MEANING OF *SÛF* AND *YAM SÛF* IN THE OLD TESTAMENT AND IN ANCIENT LITERATURE

As a common noun (as over against a proper name, *yam sûf*), the term *sûf* appears in just four biblical texts: Exodus 2:3, 5; Isaiah 19:6b; Jonah 2:5b [MT 2:6b]. Attested twice in the Pentateuch, in a single context, the word describes the place where the infant Moses was laid along the bank of the Nile. The text reads:

> But when she [i.e., the mother of Moses] could hide him no longer, she got a *papyrus basket* [*tēbat gōmeʾ*[1]] for him and

---

1. Both Egyptian loanwords. See BDB, 167, 1061; *HALOT*, 196; 1678; *DCH* 8:585.

FIGURE 1: **Reeds on bank of Nile River**

Reeds/rushes pictured here flourish at certain places along the Nile River and in adjacent zones. The mother of Moses is said to have put her infant son into a papyrus basket and to have placed the basket among the reeds along the bank of the Nile (Exod 2:3). (Photo by Güldem Üstün, via Flickr, under CC BY 2.0)

coated it [*taḥmərāh²*] with *tar* [*ḥamār³*] and *pitch* [*zāpet⁴*]. Then she placed the child in it and put it among the *reeds* [*sûf⁵*] along the bank of the *Nile* [*yə'ōr⁶*]. (Exod 2:3 NIV; emphasis added)

Two verses later we are informed that the daughter of the *pharaoh* (*par'ōh;* Egyptian loanword) went down to the Nile to bathe; she saw the "basket" (again, *tēbâ*) among the "reeds" (again, *sûf*, no textual variants) and retrieved it (Exod 2:5).

---

2. Cognate with an Egyptian root. See BDB, 330; *HALOT*, 331; *DCH* 3:258.

3. Same root as in the previous note.

4. Cognate with Egyptian root. See BDB, 278; *HALOT*, 277; *DCH* 3:129.

5. There are no textual variants. The word refers to some sort of water plant.

6. An Egyptian loanword.

It is important to recognize a very strong, pronounced Egyptian lexical and linguistic presence in this brief passage, employing common nouns of a narrow focus and semitechnical nature. Moreover, all of these terms (with the exception of the proper names Nile and pharaoh) are nearly nonexistent throughout the remainder of the Old Testament canon. Here in this one remarkably short paragraph, however, we find a concentration of eight such lexemes (italicized above; three used twice), all directly related to the Egyptian language and to Egyptian culture. This is a significant and inescapable conclusion (see below).[7]

Similarly, as in this Exodus text, the usage of *sûf* in Isaiah points to some sort of plant/botanical designation inside Egypt. The text is

---

7. It is worthwhile to notice that later in this same paragraph (2:10), the name Moses (*mōšeh*) is assigned. Assuming the nearest pronominal antecedents "her (son)" and "she (named)" in this verse to be the daughter of the pharaoh (also note "*I* drew him out"), this would also appear to be an Egyptian loanword brought into Hebrew (cf. Richard S. Hess, "Onomastics of the Exodus Generation in the Book of Exodus," in Hoffmeier, Millard, and Rendsburg, *"Did I Not Bring Israel Out of Egypt?,"* 37–39, who considers it more likely that "Moses" is of West Semitic origin). Were the root to be Semitic in character, it should be noted that it is otherwise attested in the Hebrew text with extremely low frequency, apparently only in one synoptic passage (2 Sam 22:17//Ps 18:16 [MT 18:17]; BDB, 602; HALOT, 642; Dewey M. Beegle, "Moses (Person): Old Testament," *ABD* 4:911). However, this word is repeatedly found in other Egyptian personal names (e.g., Kamose/Kamosis ["the bull is born"]; Ahmose/Ahmosis ["(the lunar god) Iah is born," given to two different NK kings]; Thutmose/Thutmosis ["(the lunar god) Thoth is born," assigned to four different NK kings]; and Rameses ["(the solar god) Ra' is born," selected for eleven different NK kings]; consult Ronald J. Leprohon, *The Great Name: Ancient Egyptian Royal Titulary*, WAW 33 [Atlanta: Society of Biblical Literature, 2013] 91–123; cf. BDB, 602; HALOT, 642–43). One must also bear in mind the relevant fact that a number of toponyms located inside Egypt and found in the early exodus narratives are similarly attested in contemporary Egyptian literature and also appear to be of Egyptian extraction: (1) Pithom [pi(r)-(I)tum, "house of (the Egyptian god) Atum"]; (2) Rameses [pi(r)-Rameses, "house of Ra'"]; (3) Succoth [Egyptian *tjeku/t̠-k-w*], the Egyptian name of a city and perhaps also a region in the Wadi Tumilat (see Yoshiyuki Muchiki, *Egyptian Proper Names and Loanwords in North-West Semitic*, SBLDS 173 [Atlanta: Society of Biblical Literature, 1999], 232–33), located to the east of Pithom (*COS* 3.4.17) and a distance of one day's travel east of Rameses (*COS* 3.4.16)]; and possibly (4) Etham (Atum, so Manfred Görg, "Etam und Pitom," *BN* 51 [1980]: 9–10; Muchiki, *Egyptian Proper Names*, 230); and (5) Goshen (*g-s-m*, see Sarah I. Groll, "The Egyptian Background of the Exodus and the Crossing of the Reed Sea: A New Reading of Papyrus Anastasi VIII," in *Jerusalem Studies in Egyptology*, ed. Irene Shirun-Grumach, ÄAT 40 [Wiesbaden: Harrassowitz, 1998], 189–91, and note that no cognate verb of Goshen is found in the Hebrew Old Testament). As might be expected, this rather prominent lexical trend related to the Egyptian language discontinues after Israel's deliverance at *yam sûf*, thereby effectively departing the territory of Egypt proper and entering the realm of "wilderness."

referencing a judgment that will occur to the plant growth along the Nile, in a revealing, somewhat graphic poetic format. The prophet states:

> The canals [nəhārôt] [of the delta] will become foul smelling [zānâ⁸];
> the branches of the Lower Nile [yə'ōrê māṣôr⁹] will diminish and dry up.
> The spice reeds [qāneh] and the rushes [sûf¹⁰] will rot away; all the sown plant growth along the Nile [kōl mizra' yə'ôr] ... will become parched, blow away, and be no more. (Isa 19:6–7)

Finally, the word sûf is correspondingly employed by Jonah. As he reflects on his earlier ordeal in the depths of the Mediterranean Sea, the prophet's poetic declaration is found in the following diagnostic tricolon:

> (1) waters gathered round [lit. encompassed] my life/neck [nepeš];

> (2) the deep [təhôm] surrounded me;

> (3) seaweed [sûf¹¹] got wrapped around my head. (Jonah 2:5b [MT/LXX 2:6b])

From their translation of these texts in the LXX, it is clear the Jewish scholars were well aware of a semantic field for sûf that related to water plants commonly known to exist at various places and especially along the Nile.[12] Thus, for example, both Exodus LXX citations are rendered helos (apparently in context referencing either a marshy area or some associated type of water plant, bulrush, cattail, reed,

---

8. See BDB, 276; HALOT, 276.

9. See also Exod 7:18; 8:1.

10. There are no textual variants.

11. There are no textual variants.

12. On water plants mentioned in the Old Testament, see Irene Jacob and Walter Jacob, "Flora," ABD 2:814.

sedge, punk, or the like), and the text of Isaiah 19:6 is translated *kala-mos*[13] ("reed" or "paper-reed" of some sort).[14]

Accordingly, the notion of interpreting the MT vocable *sûf* in a botanical sense goes back in Jewish tradition at least as far as the pre-Christian era and the LXX. Such an understanding is also consistently reflected in Christian Bibles produced over the past eight hundred years (and since the Reformation, in Protestant and Catholic versions alike), and both historic and contemporary scholarship generally concur with such an assessment (see below, note 32). However, in vivid contradistinction to this virtually unanimous studied scholarly conviction, Fritz confidently asserts otherwise, denying any possible botanical meaning to the word *sûf*.[15] Questioning their justification, Fritz declares that botanical translations are "statistical outliers" and

---

13. More specifically, the LXX text reads "every marshy area [*helos*] of reeds [*kalamos*] and papyrus [*papyros*] will rot away." The Greek word *kalamos* is later associated with the crucifixion of Jesus (Matt 27:29; Mark 15:19; perhaps referring to "cattails").

14. It is difficult to determine how *sûf* is being rendered in LXX Jonah 2:6b, if at all. The poetic tricolon appears as follows (and compare the MT tricolon just above):

(1) "water poured around me to the soul [*psychē*];
(2) the lowest/farthest deep [*abyssos ... eschatos*] surrounded me;
(3) my head went down to the bottom [lit. schism] of the mountains [*schism horos*]."

Clearly, Hebrew *nepeš* and Greek *psychē* are corresponding poetic elements in the first line, and it appears that *təhôm* and *abyssos/eschatos* function in the same way in the second line (understanding *eschatos* adjectivally; so Ellis Brotzman and Raymond Martin, *Jonah: Computer Generated Tools for the Study of Correlated Greek and Hebrew Texts of the Old Testament* [Wooster, OH: Biblical Research Associates, 1998], 77, 158). If that were the case, then accounting for *sûf* in the LXX remains a vexed consideration. It is argued that *sûf* may be poetically represented in the rendering *eschatos* ("the lowest/farthest" [deep]). Thus, e.g., Bernard F. Batto, "The Reed Sea: *Requiescat in Pace*," *JBL* 102.1 (1983): 27–35; Batto, "Mythic Dimensions of the Exodus Tradition," in Levy, Schneider, and Propp, *Israel's Exodus in Transdisciplinary Perspective*, 187–95, who wishes to repoint *sûp* to *sôp* and to see here a reference to a mythical sea situated at the farthest edge of the world. A broad sweep of recent commentaries continue to argue for understanding *sûf* in a botanical sense in Jonah, related to the other Old Testament usages: thus, e.g., Hans Walter Wolff, *Obadiah and Jonah: A Commentary*, trans. Margaret Kohl, CC (Minneapolis: Augsburg, 1987), 136, huge algae; Meir Zlotowitz, *Jonah: A New Translation with a Commentary Anthologized from Talmudic, Midrashic and Rabbinic Sources*, ArtScroll Tanach (Brooklyn: Mesorah, 1978), 113, weeds; Douglas Stuart, *Hosea-Jonah*, WBC 31 (Waco, TX: Word Books, 1987), 469, seaweed; Jack M. Sasson, *Jonah: A New Translation with Introduction, Commentary, and Interpretation*, AB 24B (New York: Doubleday, 1990), 182–85, kelp; James Limburg, *Jonah: A Commentary*, OTL (Louisville: Westminster John Knox, 1993), 94, reeds.

15. Fritz, *Lost Sea of Exodus* (2016), 163–66, 183.

"seem like sloppy approximations."[16] He makes the following claim: "Based on historical review and basic vocabulary analysis, these botanical terms amount to traditional interpretations rather than rigorous, literal translations."[17] Fritz wants to translate *sûf* in both Exodus citations "pool/basin," the Isaiah text as "banks," and he renders the Jonah reference "sea floor."[18] However, Isaiah applies to *sûf* the verbs "to rot" (*qāmal*), "to become foul smelling" (*zānâ*), "to diminish" (*dālal*), and "to dry up" (*ḥārab*), which collectively argue conclusively against his "banks" gloss. Similarly, Jonah applies to *sûf* the verbs "to wrap around" (*ḥābaš*), "to encompass" (*'āpap*), and "to surround" (*sābab*), which all invalidate his "sea floor" understanding. His work at this point tacitly disregards both recognized Hebrew and LXX lexicography and the hermeneutical essence of Hebrew parallelism found in a poetic structure. At the end of the day, it must be recognized that Fritz's conceptual idiosyncrasies are governing his claim here, for he believes if he can eliminate any botanical nuance for the lexeme *sûf*, his corollary case for rejecting "Reed/Papyrus Sea" as a possible translation of *yam sûf* has been firmly established.[19]

Let me begin my response to Fritz by identifying this assertion for what it is: An astonishing and sweeping philological and lexical judgment of the first order! In an effort to anchor his novel assertion, Fritz relies on two sources: Wilhelm Gesenius and James Strong, both of whom he seems to misinterpret. Let me explain. To begin with, Fritz quotes a section from a noun entry of *sûf* in Gesenius, where the highly acclaimed Hebrew authority states: "rush, reed, sea weed. The etymology is not known, and it cannot be derived from the verb סוף [*swf*]."[20] It appears that Fritz wrongly reads Gesenius to be saying that since the noun *sûf*—found in the four biblical texts cited just above

---

16. Fritz, *Lost Sea of Exodus* (2016), 164.

17. Fritz, *Lost Sea of Exodus* (2016), 163.

18. Fritz, *Lost Sea of Exodus* (2016), 167–69.

19. Fritz, "Lost Sea of Exodus" (2006), 14–15; Fritz, *Lost Sea of Exodus* (2016), 8.

20. Fritz, *Lost Sea of Exodus* (2016), 163. Quotation taken from Wilhelm Gesenius, *Gesenius' Hebrew and Chaldee Lexicon to the Old Testament Scripture* (Grand Rapids: Baker, 1979), 581.

and construed in botanical terms—apparently bears no etymological connection to the Hebrew verb *swf*, one must look elsewhere beyond botany to find meaning for this noun that is in conformity with the etymology of the verb, which means "to come to an end, to cease."

In point of fact, one notes that Gesenius's stated meanings for this noun—"rush, reed, sea weed"—are strictly of a botanical nature. Moreover, as one reads further in Gesenius's lexical entry, beyond the part quoted by Fritz, the esteemed Hebrew scholar cites three of the texts under review here (Exod 2:3, 5; Isa 19:6) and translates them "a rush growing in the Nile," and with respect to the Jonah passage, Gesenius offers "sea weed." In fact, even in earlier editions of Gesenius, these same botanical translational options are offered (with no nonbotanical options listed), in the context of all four verses under consideration here, and Gesenius also wrestles there with the etymology of *sûf*, offering the possibility of a lexical connection with Egyptian *twfi*.[21] This is actually a quite remarkable insight made by Gesenius in the mid-1800s, before most of the Egyptian *twf* textual evidence had been published. Not surprisingly, in Gesenius's research found in BDB, the point is likewise made that the noun *sûf* used in these four texts is "probably a loan-word from Egyptian *twfi*, 'reeds.'"[22] Given the conviction that, with *sûf*, one is most likely dealing with an Egyptian loanword, it makes sense that Gesenius should have stated in the Fritz quotation above that this word "cannot be derived from the [Hebrew!] verb סוף [*swf*]." In any event, Gesenius consistently maintains a distinctly botanical nuance for the biblical lexeme *sûf*, precisely the opposite of the claim made by Fritz.

I move to his second source, *Strong's Exhaustive Concordance*.[23] In his table 11.1, Fritz lists nine entries from Strong that have a similar sound in Hebrew and a similar transliteration in English.[24] As

---

21. See the 1844 edition (723) and the 1866 edition (716) of Gesenius's lexicon.

22. BDB, 693.

23. James Strong, *Strong's Exhaustive Concordance* (Nashville: Nelson, 1990).

24. Fritz, *Lost Sea of Exodus* (2016), 164; see also his table 9.3 in Fritz, "Lost Sea of Exodus" (2006), 199.

it were, these words are homonyms or near homonyms. From this, however, Fritz presumably believes that similarity of phonology constitutes similarity of lexicography, arguing in effect that homonyms can easily become synonyms. He labels this table "The Biblical *Suph* Word Family," and he apparently understands these nine entries in Strong's *Concordance* to be in the same etymological family and therefore lexically interrelated. This is made explicit at one point, where Fritz declares, "A key premise of this analytical approach is that the Hebrew language consists of families of words that stem from a root word which loans its form and meaning to the entire family."[25] Anyone who works professionally in the discipline is fully aware that Strong's *Concordance* may be utilized to analyze Hebrew lexicography in no such fashion. Given such erroneous thinking, it is easy to see how Fritz might then use *any* of the nine meanings to apply to whatever text may be in view at the moment.

However, if one examines established Hebrew philological and lexicographic authorities (e.g., BDB, *HALOT*, *DCH*), one will easily discover that these nine similar-sounding entries in Strong demonstrably derive from at least four separate and discrete philological roots, which is actually a fairly natural contour in the etymological landscape when, as here, one is dealing with a weak verb, either a "hollow verb" (i.e., *√CŵC/CŷC roots), a "geminate verb" (i.e., *√CC² root), and/ or a "3rd-*he* verb" (i.e., *√CCY root). These roots appear as follows:

> (1) √sp and/or √spp—one/two Hebrew nouns, one meaning "basin, bowl, goblet, household object" (e.g., Exod 12:22; 2 Sam 17:28; 1 Kgs 7:50; 2 Kgs 12:14; Jer 52:19; Hab 2:15; Zech 12:2) and (perhaps) another noun meaning "threshold, sill, doorframe, doorkeeper" (e.g., Judg 19:27; 1 Kgs 14:17; 2 Kgs 12:10; 1 Chr 9:19; 2 Chr 3:7; 34:9; Isa 6:4; Ezek 40:6; 41:16; Amos 9:1).[26]

---

25. Fritz, "Lost Sea of Exodus" (2006), 198.

26. Strong #5592; BDB, 706; *HALOT*, 762–63 (and see philological note on 765); *DCH* 6:176–77, 182. It is pertinent to consider a probable Akkadian lexemic analogy in this regard: (1)

(2) √*sph*—a Hebrew verb meaning "to take away, to carry away, to sweep away; to snatch away" (e.g., Gen 19:15–17; Num 16:26; Ps 40:14 [MT 40:15]; Prov 13:23).[27]

(3) √*swp* or √*sûp*—a Hebrew verb meaning "to come to an end; to cease, to end" (e.g., 1 Sam 15:33; Ps 73:19; Isa 66:17; Amos 3:15; Zeph 1:2) and a cognate Hebrew noun meaning "an end, a rearguard" (e.g., 2 Chr 20:16; Eccl 7:2b; Joel 2:20).[28]

(4) √*sûf*—a probable Egyptian loanword (noun), meaning "reeds, rushes, seaweed" (e.g., Exod 2:3, 5, Isa 19:6b; Jonah 2:5b [MT 2:6b]).[29]

I submit that here is a case in which misusing English language tools to attempt to understand Hebrew philology has led Fritz into a far-reaching, fatally misguided hermeneutical error. One must recognize this as exegetical frivolity, based on no lexical source(s) but rather exclusively on his own preconceived and wishful ideology. No convincing lexicographical or etymological objection can be raised to the long-standing and widely held conviction that the biblical common noun *sûf* should be construed in some sort of a botanical sense and is most likely to be philologically related to Egyptian *ṯwf* (or *ṯwfy*), also understood to possess a direct botanical denotation, perhaps a papyrus plant, a marsh plant, and/or a watery marsh.[30]

---

sappu [A], "a basket, container, (metal) object" [*AHw*, 1027; *CAD* 15, s.v. "sappu A"], or its variant *šappu*, "a household container" [*AHw*, 1175; *CAD* 17.1, s.v. "šappu"]; as over against (2) *sippu* [A], "a doorpost, doorframe, doorjamb, entrance(way)" [*AHw*, 1049; *CAD* 15, s.v. "sippu A"].

27. Strong #5595; BDB, 705; HALOT, 763–64; DCH 6:178–79.

28. Strong ##5486, 5487, 5490, 5491, 5492(?); BDB, 692–93; HALOT, 746–47; DCH 6:133–34.

29. Strong ##5488, 5489; BDB, 693; HALOT, 747; DCH 6:134.

30. A still beneficial discussion of the possible meanings of *ṯwf* can be found in William A. Ward, "The Semitic Biconsonantal Root *SP* and the Common Origin of Egyptian ČWF and Hebrew SÛP: 'Marsh(-Plant),'" *VT* 24 (1974): 339–49. Moreover, it is noteworthy to observe that the Egyptian word *ṯwf* can in context be further qualified and identified semantically, with the addition of a botanical semantic classifier, with a semantic classifier that seems to

I return to my earlier discussion of *sûf* and *yam sûf* in Exodus 2 and in ancient literature. Given the conspicuous concentration of overtly Egyptian lexicography found in the aforementioned paragraph relating to the birth, naming, and early adoption of Moses (Exod 2:1–10), it is not surprising that leading Egyptological and biblical scholars have long recognized a direct linguistic and lexical connection between the MT word *sûf* and the corresponding Egyptian word *ṯwf(y)*.[31] The Egyptian lexeme *ṯwf* (or *ṯwfy*, sometimes written with the definite article *pꜣ-ṯwf*) is found in five diagnostically revealing New Kingdom papyri, where it designates a geographical entity, a lush region and/or a defined area, situated presumably along the easternmost edge of the Nile Delta.[32] The region of *(pꜣ)-ṯwf* is one of

---

speak of a watery region, and/or with an added toponymic semantic classifier. An extremely helpful discussion of the various uses of water plants in ancient Egypt may be found in Jacob and Jacob, "Flora," 814–15.

31. For the Egyptian phoneme *ṯ* (sometimes transcribed *tj* or *č* in English) = Hebrew *s*, refer to James E. Hoch, *Semitic Words In Egyptian Texts of the New Kingdom and Third Intermediate Period* (Princeton: Princeton University Press, 1994), 364–75; cf. for the equation applied specifically to place names, see Anson F. Rainey, "Toponymic Problems (cont.)," *TA* 9 (1982): 133–34.

32. (1) Papyrus Sallier (I:4, 9; BM10185; see Alan H. Gardiner, *Late-Egyptian Miscellanies* [Brussels: Édition de la Fondation égyptologique reine Élisabeth, 1937], 80–82; Ricardo A. Caminos, *Late-Egyptian Miscellanies* [London: Oxford University Press, 1954], 303; *LAE* 343); (2) Papyrus Anastasi III (2:11–12; BM10246; see Gardiner, *Late-Egyptian Miscellanies*, 22–23; Caminos, *Late-Egyptian Miscellanies*, 73–82 [cf. *ANET*, 471; *COS* 3.3.15]); (3) Papyrus Anastasi IV (15.6; BM10249; see Gardiner, *Late-Egyptian Miscellanies*, 49–52; Caminos, *Late-Egyptian Miscellanies*, 198–219); (4) Papyrus Anastasi VIII (rev 3.3–4; BM10248; see *RITA* 3:354–56 [#228]; Groll, "Egyptian Background," 173–92); and (5) Onomasticon of Amenope (#418; see *AEO* 2:198–204, and consult his "Lower Egypt" sketch map).

In accordance with the LXX translation, the tendency to read biblical *sûf* in a botanical sense and *yam sûf* as a lexically related (proper) name (a defined area, region, and perhaps even a toponym) stretches far back in Jewish and Christian traditions. Thus, e.g., Aquila used *papureon* to translate *sûf* in Exod 2:3, 5. Jerome, *Epistulae* 78.9 [*Ad Fabiolam*]) translated *yam sûf* as "a swamp/lake where rushes are plentiful." The eleventh century biblical exegete and renowned Talmudic scholar Rashi, as part of his interpretation of Exod 2, 13, and Isa 19, offered this comment: "The word *sup* has the meaning of a marshy tract in which reeds grow"; see S. Bamberger, ed., *Raschi's Pentateuchkommentar = Rashi 'al ha-Torah* (Hamburg: Kramer, 1928), 173–74, 416, 456. Such an interpretation of *yam sûf* is reflected in an important sixteenth century German Bible translation (Martin Luther, *Lutherbibel*, 1534, "Reed Sea;" see also John Wycliffe's Bible in c. 1382, "Reed sea") as well as in a highly influential Latin translation (Immanuel Tremellius, Franciscus Junius, and Theodore Beza, *Biblia Sacra*, 1590, "sedgy sea of reeds"). Likewise, in a sixteenth century map of Abraham Ortelius, *Theatrum orbis terrarium* (Antwerp: van Diest, 1570), 8:12, map 8) one reads: "The Arabian Gulfe (is) called of the Greeks ἐρυθραῖα θάλασση, *Mare rubrum* the red sea: of the Hebrewes יַם־סוּף *iam-suff, mare algosum vel iuncosum* the sedgie

the verdant areas in the vicinity of Rameses celebrated for providing foodstuffs and other supplies to the capital city. In one instance the best green fodder for the royal horses is said to have been supplied by *pꜣ-ṯwf* (the word occurs with added botanical, watery, and town semantic classifiers); in another instance the region of *ṯwf* (no definite article) supplied a certain species of bird (the word occurs with an added botanical and town semantic classifier). We are told in another text that cargo vessels with papyrus reeds and rushes aboard were being sent to Rameses from the eastern delta from the *pꜣ-ṯwf* region (the word occurs with an added botanical semantic classifier), and in yet another text the scribe appears to be concerned lest a supply barge from the east is sent to Rameses but having aboard no rushes/reeds from the *pꜣ-ṯwf* region (see map 2).

Perhaps it is the late Twentieth Dynasty text Onomasticon of Amenope that offers the most clarifying contextual information. This papyrus contains an enumeration of over six hundred named entities, listed by category, such as the names of (1) kings and other high officials (entries 63–229); (2) various people groups (entries 230–312);

sea: of the Arabians the neere inhabitants *Bahci 'lkuzom* the alkulzom sea." On his "Aegyptus Antiqua" map in this same volume, Ortelius denotes the modern Red Sea as follows: *ARABICI SINUS PARS, Hebraei MARE SUPH nominant BRACHIA etiam dicitur Stephano Oriens*" [*mare algosum*], "Iter Israelitarum" map: סוף ים, *Mare Algae*. Note that Samuel Bochart, *Geographia Sacra, seu Phaleg et Canaan* (Leiden: Boutesteyn & Luchtmans, 1692), 283, had embraced a similar conviction based on Hesychius (see Mauricius Schmidt, *Hesychii Alexandrini Lexicon* [Jenae: Maukiana, 1864], col. 1261 [§2893]), who speaks of *hē thalassa, hē polu phykion echousa* ["a sea that contains much seaweed"]). Heinrich Karl Brugsch, *Hieroglyphisch-Demotisches Wörterbuch* (Leipzig: Hinrichs, 1868), 4.1580–81), was the first to make a direct lexical connection between MT *sûf* and Egyptian *ṯwf*, followed by F. Max Müller ("A Contribution to the Exodus Geography," *PSBA* 10 [1888]: 474–77). Adolf Erman and Hermann Grapow (*Wörterbuch der ägyptischen Sprache*, 5 vols. [Berlin: Akademie, 1926–1963; repr., 1982], 5/1:359 [6–10]) sought to establish *sûf* as an Egyptian loanword, an equation that has been embraced by a wide array of leading Egyptological experts, including such names as Alan Gardiner, Ricardo Caminos, William Kelly Simpson, Edward Wente, Sarah Groll, Kenneth Kitchen, Anson Rainey, Manfred Bietak, and James Hoffmeier. Consult also Thomas O. Lambdin, "Egyptian Loan Words in the Old Testament," *JAOS* 73 (1953): 153; Muchiki, *Egyptian Proper Names*, 251–52; Aaron D. Rubin, "Egyptian Loanwords," *EHLL* 1:793–94; Benjamin J. Noonan, "Egyptian Loanwords as Evidence for the Authenticity of the Exodus and Wilderness Traditions," in Hoffmeier, Millard, and Rendsburg, *Did I Not Bring Israel Out of Egypt?*, 51–57. It is thus unclear to me how Fritz can argue that the concept "sea of reeds" only emerged as a synonym for the Red Sea in the Renaissance period (Fritz, *Lost Sea of Exodus* [2016], 76).

(3) different kinds of land (entries 420–578); and a few other categories. Near the middle of this text, one finds listed a category of slightly
more than one hundred town names of Upper and Lower Egypt,
understood to be sequentially presented in a south to north pattern,
following the direction of the flow of the Nile (listed in the papyrus
as entries 313–419). A number of these town listings can be unas-
sailably identified with modern sites, including Kom Ombo (listed
as #316); Silsilah (#317); Edfu (#322); Dendara (#343); Lycopolis
(#371); Speos Artemidos (#381); Memphis (#394); Cairo (#397A);
Heliopolis (#400); Tell el-Yahudiya (#401); Tell el-Farʿûn (#409);
Pi-Rameses (#410); Tell el-Balamun (#413); Tanis (#417), and others.
Immediately following Tanis one finds the entry *pȝ-ṯwf* (#418, written with an added town semantic classifier, indicating a place name,
in a list of place names).[33] Just after this entry, the final toponymic
entry in the listing is given, the site of Tjaru/Sile (= T. Hebua, #419).
Situated therefore near to Tanis/Zoan (#417) and Tjaru/Sile (#419),[34]
the toponym/defined area *pȝ-ṯwf* (#418) must have been located near
the edge of the easternmost segment of the Nile Delta, on the very
border of Egypt.[35]

---

33. Consult in this regard Manfred Bietak, "On the Historicity of the Exodus: What
Egyptology Today Can Contribute to Assessing the Biblical Account of the Sojourn in Egypt,"
in Levy, Schneider, and Propp, *Israel's Exodus in Transdisciplinary Perspective*, 27.

34. See map 2 on page 35 for the placement of both sites.

35. The fact that the name *pȝ-ṯwf(y)* appears twice in a much later (first century AD demotic)
papyrus, again unambiguously as a toponym and in a context that points toward the easternmost region of the delta, provides some sense of an extended use of the name as a defined area,
beyond the New Kingdom period only, nearer to the time when the LXX was translated (see
Galit Dayan, "The Term '*pȝ-ṯwf*' in the Spiegelberg Papyrus," in Shirun-Grumach, *Jerusalem
Studies in Egyptology*, 134). Had the LXX translators been aware of such a lush Egyptian geographical entity (an area, a watery region, and/or perhaps even a place name [cf. *tjeku/ṯ-k-w*//
Succoth, clearly referenced both as a region and as a toponym; cf. Hans G. Goedicke, "Tjeku,"
LÄ 6 col 609]), this could explain, conceptually speaking, the idea of hyphenating the Hebrew
word *yām* to the proper name *pȝ-ṯwf*, thus identifying by name a body of water contiguous
to the entity (**yam-[pȝ]-ṯwf > yam-sûf*). This has precedent in the site of Kinnereth (Khirbet
el-ʿOreima; Tel Kinrot), a small and seemingly insignificant village located about 2.25 miles (3.6
km) west of Capernaum and adjacent to the Sea of Galilee. The site of Kinnereth is mentioned
in the OT, listed as a town that formed part of the territorial inheritance of the tribe of Naphtali
(Josh 19:35; cf. Deut 3:17; 1 Kgs 15:20), but its name was also lent to the body of water to which
the site was adjacent (*yam-Kinnereth*, e.g. Num 34:11; Josh 12:3; 13:27).

FIGURE 2: **Rice paddy fields near Rameses/Qantir**

A field of rice paddies planted adjacent to the biblical site of Rameses/Qantir reflects even today the lush fertility of the immediate vicinity of the ancient Egyptian capital. (Photo by Barry J. Beitzel)

2.2 A "THREE-DAY" CONSIDERATION

The near proximity of the Re(e)d Sea event to Egypt also appears to be reflected almost as a theme in Moses' exchange with the pharaoh. Thus, for example, while still near Mt. Sinai, Moses is given instructions concerning what he and the elders should say when they first approach the Egyptian king and ask him to "let Israel go." They were told to declare the following: "The LORD, the God of the Hebrews, has met with us. Let us take a **three-day journey** *into the wilderness*[36] to offer sacrifices to the LORD our God" (Exod 3:18). Pharaoh's initial refusal was met with another request of an almost verbatim nature: "Let us take a **three-day journey** *into the wilderness* to offer sacrifices to the LORD our God" (Exod 5:3). Later, in the midst of the plagues and in an effort to have Moses remove the swarming flies, the pharaoh offers Moses a compromise: "You may go and offer sacrifices

---

36. Hebrew *midbār*, rendered either "wilderness" or "desert" in the versions.

to your God here *in the land* [of Egypt]." To this Moses responds with
a question: "If we were to offer sacrifices that were anathema to the
Egyptians, right before their very eyes, would they not stone us?"
Moses then continues, "We must take a **three-day journey** *into the
wilderness* to offer sacrifices to the LORD, our God." With no viable
alternative, the pharaoh temporarily relents and states: "Okay, you
may go *into the wilderness* to offer sacrifices, but don't go very far"
(Exod 8:25–28 [MT 8:21–25], emphases added throughout).[37]

Two relevant patterns emerge from these texts: First, what is italicized just above points to a mutually exclusive and recurring binary
theme between "the land of Egypt" (where there are Egyptians present) and "the wilderness" (an area located a safe distance beyond the
range of Egyptian cultic holiness, where any passing Egyptian presence would not serve as a deterrent to genuine Israelite worship; see
also 5:1b; 7:1).[38] Second, from what is in bold above, it seems clear,
for Israel to travel as far as the wilderness would constitute about
a three-day venture. And since one of Moses' demands to "let the
people go" definitely took place at the pharaoh's palace at Rameses
(8:25), as presumably is the case with the encounter in 5:3, one might

---

37. Attempts to vitiate and easily jettison a three-day consideration are sometimes predi-
cated on the assumption that the destination involved in Moses' request was Mt. Sinai, though
that is neither stated nor implied in the biblical text. To the contrary, it seems plausible to
understand this as a rather straightforward appeal, and to assume it was a petition to be granted
time away from work "to hold a festival [to Yahweh] in the [proximate] wilderness" (cf. Exod
3:18; 5:1–3; see also 5:8, 17; 7:16; 8:27). To judge from the pharaoh's own proposal in this regard
(Exod 8:25; cf. 8:8b) or from his response to Moses' counterproposal (8:28), this is arguably the
way in which the Egyptian monarch himself understood the request. Such a petition would have
been very much in line with what we otherwise know of New Kingdom brickmaking practices,
in which workers at various tiers were sometimes permitted time off "to worship (their) god" or
to have idle time "for a religious festival" (for the relevant evidentiary documentation, consult
Kenneth A. Kitchen, *Ancient Orient and Old Testament* [Downers Grove, IL: InterVarsity, 1966],
156–57; Kitchen, "From the Brickyards of Egypt," *TynBul* 27 [1976]: 145–46; Kitchen, *On the
Reliability of the Old Testament* [Grand Rapids: Eerdmans, 2003], 248–49, 553n10; refer also
to James K. Hoffmeier, *Israel in Egypt: The Evidence for the Authenticity of the Exodus Tradition*
[New York: Oxford, 1996], 112–15). See now *RITA* 2:519–26 (#283); 3:361–68 (#A.15).

38. Refer to details found in Barry J. Beitzel, "Israel's Forty Years in the Wilderness: A
Geographic and Socio-spatial Analysis," in *Lexham Geographic Commentary on the Pentateuch*,
ed. Barry J. Beitzel (Bellingham, WA: Lexham, forthcoming).

FIGURE 3: **Brick structure at Tell er-Retaba**

Enslaved while in Egypt, Israelites were forced to work fields and to make bricks (Exod 1:13–14; 5:7) for the construction of the vast Egyptian capital city, Rameses, as well as a number of surrounding towns, including the site of Pithom/Tell er-Retaba (Exod 1:11). Pictured here is the vestige of buildings and a wall made of mud-brick construction from this same period, discovered at Tell er-Retaba. (Photo by Barry J. Beitzel)

conclude that the Egyptian capital itself lay at an approximate distance of three-days' journey from the edge of the wilderness.

A wider exegetical analysis of the expression "three days" or "the third day" may be in order here. This expression occurs nearly fifty times in the Old Testament. A wide majority of these citations convey a temporal designation:

- Gen 22:4—Traveling presumably from Beersheba, Abraham sees Mt. Moriah on the third day of his journey.

- Gen 40:12—Joseph declares that within three days the imprisoned Egyptian butler will be restored to his previous post (note the relationship between three baskets and three days).

- Gen 40:18—Joseph declares that within three days the Egyptian baker will lose his life (note the additional reference to the "third day").

- Gen 42:17–18—Joseph imprisons his brothers for a period of three days.

- Exod 15:22; Num 33:8—Israel travels three days in the wilderness.

- Num 19:12–19—Unclean persons are to be cleansed with water on the third day (note the additional references to the "seventh day").

- Josh 1:11; Esth 4:15—Israel is to consecrate itself for three days, before a significant event (in connection with the Joshua text, refer also to 3:2; note the Esther text specifies three days and nights; see also Ezra 8:32–33, and see the additional reference to the "fourth day").

- Josh 2:16, 22—Spies are to hide themselves in the hills west of Jericho for three days.

- Judg 14:14—Samson's riddle cannot be interpreted in three days (note the additional reference to the "fourth day").

- Judg 19:4—The Levite stays for three days in the house of his concubine's father (note the additional reference to the "fourth day" and the "fifth day").

- 1 Sam 9:20—Saul spends three days searching for his father's asses.

- 2 Sam 1:2—David remains in Ziklag for two days, but on the third day, a man from Saul's camp approaches.

- 2 Sam 24:13//1 Chr 21:12—David's choices of punishment for his census include three days of pestilence in the land.

- 2 Kgs 20:5—After being healed, Hezekiah is to go to the temple on the third day.

- 1 Kgs 12:12// 2 Chr 10:5—The men of Israel who appeal to Rehoboam for a less burdensome yoke are told to return in three days for his final answer.

- Jonah 1:17 [MT 2:1]—Jonah is said to have spent three days and three nights in the large fish.

The expression in all these contexts appears to be understood temporally, and in a rather literal sense, one that is either clearly implied or strongly suggested. I can find no clear exceptions to this understanding.

Beyond these citations, there are three important texts where the designation may be either temporal, or spatial, or both. Moreover, one notes that these three texts juxtapose the same distinctive phraseology with "three days" also found in the three Exodus citations in question here. In the first of these texts (Gen 30:36), we are told that Laban separated his spotted/speckled flock of sheep and goats from his plain flock by a safe "distance of three days" (Heb: *derek* + three days). In another text (Num 10:33), we are told that the Israelites were separated from the ark of the covenant by the "distance of three days" (Heb: *derek* + three days). In the final citation (Jonah 3:3), Jonah is said to have gone to Nineveh, a city described as "three days' journey in breadth" (Heb: *hālak* + three days).

It is significant in this regard to observe the similar distinctive wording in Exodus (3:18; 5:3; 8:27 [MT 8:23]—*hālak* + *derek* + three days + wilderness). All three of these other texts are understood in commentary literature either in a temporal or a spatial sense, but in either case the respective interpretation seems to be grounded in a rather literal meaning of the number, not in some hyperbolic or idiomatic sense.[39] And by way of analogy, in the same way that Laban's two flocks were separated a safe distance, or that the Israelites and the ark were to be separated a safe distance, so in Exodus it appears the Egyptians and the Israelites needed to be separated by a safe distance (whether construed temporally or spatially), so that Israel could safely worship the Lord, in what might be regarded in these texts as functional separation. In light of this, and combined with the aforementioned binary linkage between Egypt//wilderness, it seems reasonable to conclude that the conversations between Moses and the pharaoh entail a rather literal intelligibility and are therefore describing events that would take place in the wilderness, just beyond Egyptian control, but in close proximity to Egypt.

This conclusion appears to be borne out with additional consideration. When finally the moment arrived when the Israelites were to be liberated from their slavery, we are told they journeyed first "from Rameses to Succoth" (Exod 12:37; Num 33:5); then they moved on "from Succoth to Etham, on the edge [*qaṣēh*, see below] of the wilderness" (Exod 13:20; Num 33:6–8a); from there they turned/veered (*šûb*) and camped "in front of Pi-hahiroth," which was adjacent to the sea (Exod 14:2) or that they turned/veered "before Migdol" which was adjacent ('al-panê) to the sea (Num 33:7b). And immediately following this in both narratives, the Israelites safely pass through the waters of deliverance and enter "the wilderness" (Exod 15:22; Num 33:8a). In other words, an actual three-day trek appears to have obtained for the Israelites on their journey between Rameses and *yam sûf* and the wilderness: day one (Rameses to Succoth), day two (Succoth to Etham), day three (Etham to Pi-hahiroth/Migdol/ *yam sûf*/wilderness).

39. See Zlotowitz, *Jonah*, 120–21; Leslie C. Allen, *The Books of Joel, Obadiah, Jonah and Micah*, NICOT (Grand Rapids: Eerdmans, 1976), 221–22; John H. Walton, *Jonah*, Bible Study Commentary (Grand Rapids: Zondervan, 1982), 37–39; John R. Kohlenberger III, *Jonah and Nahum* (Chicago: Moody Press, 1984), 58–59; Sasson, *Jonah*, 229–31; James Bruckner, *Jonah, Nahum, Habakkuk, Zephaniah*, NIVAC (Grand Rapids: Zondervan, 2004), 90.

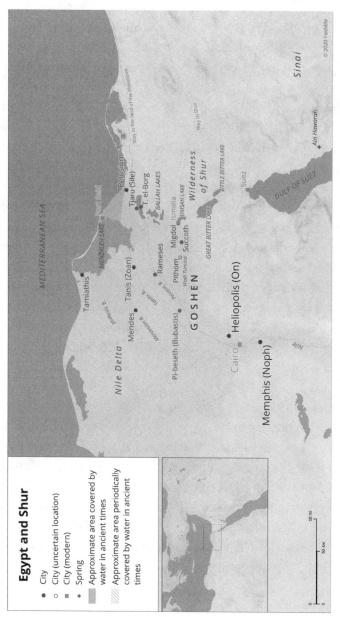

MAP 2: **Egypt and Shur**

Map of the Nile Delta and the western Sinai Peninsula

A contemporary Egyptian text is also strongly suggestive of this time frame (Papyrus Anastasi V.19.2–20.6).[40] In this New Kingdom text, a certain Egyptian troop commander reports on his assignment to pursue two runaway servants from "the king's house LPH" (i.e., Rameses, plus an added Egyptian shorthand that wishes the king and his royal household "life, prosperity, health"). The commander indicates that he had been dispatched on his retrieval mission on the evening of a specified date (3 Harvest 9, occurring in the modern month of April) and that he arrived one day later (3 Harvest 10) at the fortress of Tjeku/Succoth. Upon his arrival there, the officer was informed that the two runaways had in fact already passed that point earlier the same day. So, the commander continued his pursuit eastward toward the wilderness and came to the "wall of the Tower[41] of Seti I." When he arrived at the tower, the troop commander was advised by someone traveling in the opposite direction, westward from out of "the [Sinai] wilderness," that the fugitives had already passed that point and had fled northward. Realizing that the runaways were now safely out of Egypt and into the wilderness, thus greatly reducing the officer's likelihood of success in his mission, he abandoned his chase and reversed course.

This text seems to be relevant to the biblical account in more than one way. First, it appears that the Egyptian officer traveled from Rameses to the threshold of the wilderness in about two–three days' time. Second, one recalls that Israel's exodus itinerary—likewise undertaken in the springtime—also included the sites of Rameses–Succoth–Migdol–wilderness. I would argue the likelihood that both Israel and the Egyptian commander passed three apparently

---

40. See Gardiner, *Late-Egyptian Miscellanies*, 66–67; Kenneth A. Kitchen, "Egyptians and Hebrews, from Ra'amses to Jericho," in *The Origin of Early Israel—Current Debate: Biblical, Historical, and Archaeological Perspectives*, ed. Shmuel Aḥituv and Eliezer D. Oren, Beer-Sheva 12 (Beer-Sheva: Ben-Gurion University of the Negev Press 1998), 73–75; *COS* 3.4.16.

41. I.e., *m-k-d/t-r* = (Heb) *migdôl*; *HALOT*, 543; *DCH* 5:130–31; Erman and Grapow, *Wörterbuch der ägyptischen Sprache* 2:164; Ellen Fowles Morris, *The Architecture of Imperialism: Military Bases and the Evolution of Foreign Policy in Egypt's New Kingdom*, PAe 22 (Leiden: Brill, 2005), 417–20, 817–20.

identically named sites—and in the same sequence—within only a few days' time, before arriving at the edge of the wilderness, is too great to be coincidental. This text may well help point us to the actual course of Israel's exodus itinerary, but in any event it serves as yet another evidentiary witness that the wilderness was situated about a three-day journey from Rameses and, as a consequence, the notion that the exodus event must have occurred in rather close proximity to the eastern delta and the Wadi Tumilat is further strengthened.[42]

Finally, though this amounts only to an early tradition, it is worth noting that the first-century Jewish historian Josephus says this about the early stages of the Israelite exodus:

> They [the Israelites] took the road for Letopolis [Tell el-Yahudiya, situated in the vicinity of the land of Goshen]. ... Quitting the country by the shortest route they arrived on the third day [*tritaios*[43]] at Beelsephon [Baal-zephon], a place beside the Red Sea [*Erythras thalassēs*]. (*Ant.* 2.315 LCL)

As he continues his narration, Josephus makes clear it was from that point the "sea" (*thalatta*) was "divided" (*hypochōreō*) and Israel was "delivered" (*aphiēmi ... phugē*; 2.338), that from here Israel "left Egypt (behind)" (*kataleipō ... Aigyptos*; 2.318), and that they began to undertake their long and arduous journey through the "wilderness" (*erēmos*; 2.323).

---

42. In my view, a corresponding sequence of listed springtime stops made both by the Egyptian troop commander and by Israel—from Rameses, to Tjeku/Succoth, to Migdol, and to wilderness—mitigates against Fritz's uncorroborated countermeasure to argue on the behalf of a selectively listed biblical itinerary (Fritz, *Lost Sea of Exodus* [2016], 61–62). The question is not whether a selective or a partial listing of successive encampment stops may be found at any place along the course of Israel's entire sojourn from Egypt to Canaan, but rather whether in this immediate context there is probability that such an abridgment is being employed here, given the sequel intermediate stops made by the Egyptian commander (see below). It may also be relevant to note in this regard that whereas the stops listed in Numbers (33:5–8) are in fact found in an itinerary text, the corresponding texts in Exodus (12:37; 13:20; 14:2, 19–29) represent an essentially narrative context and not an itinerary. In other words, the consideration of the three days appears to be more than just an explicitly itinerary question.

43. The same Greek root is employed by New Testament writers to describe the day of Christ's resurrection (e.g., Matt 27:64; 1 Cor 15:4).

FIGURE 4: **Goshen and part of Wadi Tumilat**

When the family of the patriarch Jacob arrived in Egypt, the pharaoh bequeathed to them "the land of Goshen" (Gen 47:5–6), described as the best of the land of Egypt, where they would be able to eat from the fat of the land (Gen 45:18). Situated near the base of the Nile Delta and extending northeastwardly through a portion of the Wadi Tumilat, a section of the lush region of ancient Goshen is visible here. (Photo by Banja-Frans Mulder, via Wikimedia Commons, under CC BY 3.0)

In consequence of this, it seems justifiable to conclude that a three-day consideration can be said to rest upon a secure evidentiary foundation, adhering to several lines of mutually corroborating facts in the biblical text and other ancient sources, and with nothing in the text pointing unambiguously in another direction. This confluence of several evidentiary streams stands as a clear and apparent obstacle to anyone who wishes to maintain that the exodus event occurred hundreds of miles away from Egypt, somewhere in the Gulf of Aqaba/Elat.

Notwithstanding, proponents of a Gulf of Aqaba/Elat crossing point postulate what amounts to arguments of "itinerary compression" or "itinerary expansion" as a remedy. Thus, for example, as we saw just above (see page 37, footnote 42, and see my brief discussion there),

Fritz wishes to argue that the nearly identical itinerary documentation found in the historical account of the book of Exodus and in the
itinerary account of the book of Numbers is factually incomplete and
represents only a selected portion of the total number of intermediate
campsites actually visited by the people of Israel, before they finally
arrived at *yam sûf*.[44] In this case, he declares that the "biblical itinerary
allows for at least 15–20 travel days to reach the sea" (based on his
presumed average marching pace of fifteen miles [24 km] per day),
whereas only three intermediate campsites are listed in the biblical
texts (Succoth; Etham; Pi-hahiroth/Migdol [see table 2 below for a
sequence of the earliest campsites]). Thus his itinerary compression
at this point falls into the range of about 82 percent, meaning that
in his view only one in about six intermediate campsites is actually
documented in the biblical record.

Let me provide a graphic illustration of what Fritz wants us to
believe in this regard. The relevant text in Exodus 13:20 plainly reads
as follows (with no textual variations): "And they [Israel] set out
from Succoth and camped at Etham." Likewise, the parallel itineration in Numbers 33:6 reads in verbatim fashion: "And they [Israel]
set out from Succoth and camped at Etham." However, according to
the reconstruction of Fritz, these two texts must be understood and
interpreted in the following manner:

> And they [Israel] set out from Succoth and camped [at unnamed
> site #1, and then at unnamed site #2, and then at unnamed site
> #3, and then at unnamed site #4, and then at unnamed site #5,
> and then at unnamed site #6, and then] at Etham.[45]

I find it stunning that, despite calling this the "*biblical* itinerary" (my emphasis), his assessment is based entirely on the simple

44. Fritz, *Lost Sea of the Exodus* (2016), 61–62, 65.

45. It is noteworthy that Fritz cartographically displays this view and also identifies by name
and location his six proposed intermediate campsites between Succoth and Etham: El-Tasah;
Khatmia Pass; Bir Gifgafa; Bir el-Themada; Wadi el-Arish; and Wadi Misheyti. See Fritz, *Lost
Sea of the Exodus* (2016), 218–29, including fig. 14.7.

pragmatics of his own preconceived notion of where the exodus event took place, with no attempt made to provide any sort of biblical rationale or correlation in the support of his assertion.

In this regard, one must give serious attention to the exact wording repeatedly found in the biblical text, seemingly as a stereotypic formula: time after time Israel is said to have "journeyed from/set out from/broke camp at" point A ($\sqrt{ns^{c46}}$) and to have "come to/made camp at/encamped at" point B ($\sqrt{hnh^{47}}$). Then, Israel is said to "break camp at" point B and to "set up camp at" point C; and so forth (an itinerary chain, as it were). As already pointed out by Graham Davies and Angela Roskop,[48] this kind of repetitious use of place names can be found in several dozen itinerary texts from the ancient Near East, formulaically joined to words expressing linear movement, including such verbs as "to depart/proceed/set out/pitch camp/spend the night," and the like. In Assyrian itineraries, in particular, one can observe the repeated use of the verb *šakānu* ("to set up camp") and the verb *bâtu* ("to spend the night"), in the context of making sequential camp stops on a journey.[49] Likewise, one frequently finds the verb *nasāḫu* ("to set out [from camp]").[50] The first two of these verbs are the conceptual/semantic equivalents of Hebrew $\sqrt{hnh}$, and the verb *nasāḫu* is the actual lexical equivalent of Hebrew $\sqrt{ns^c}$. The presence in itineraries of such clear literary and linguistic analogies also renders an itinerary compression extremely problematic, particularly when it is employed only in the context of a circular argument.

---

46. See BDB, 652; *HALOT*, 704.

47. See BDB, 333–34; *HALOT*, 332, 1:570; and see table 2. Note some forty occurrences of this construction in the overtly itinerary presentation of Num 33 alone; but see also the analogous texts of Exod 12–19; Num 10; 12; 20–22; Deut 1; 10.

48. Graham I. Davies, *The Way of the Wilderness: A Geographical Study of the Wilderness Itineraries in the Old Testament* (Cambridge: Cambridge University Press, 1979), 56–93, 106–19; Roskop, *Wilderness Itineraries*, 50–135.

49. See *CAD* 17.1, s.v. "šakānu," see esp. 127; *CAD* 2, s.v. "bâtu."

50. *CAD* 11.2, s.v. "nasāḫu," esp. 10.

On the other hand, and as we will observe just below (see note 52), Duane Garrett[51] sets forth an argument for a daily "itinerary expansion," meaning in this case that Israel marched across the entire Sinai Peninsula—from Succoth (which he identifies with Tell el-Maskhuta) to Etham (which he speculates was located at Jebel el-Yitm, at the northern tip of the Gulf of Aqaba/Elat, and more than 220 terrestrial miles [354 km] from Succoth)—without stopping at an intermediate campsite. He declares "the angel of YHWH went before them [Israel] as a pillar of fire by night, so that they could march both day and night (13:21b)." Leaving aside the staggering distance Israel would have been required to travel in a very short time, without an encampment stop and with no indication of food or water consumed along the way, the notion of the pillar of fire deserves to be explored more fully.[52]

---

51. Garrett, *Commentary on Exodus*, 384-85; strangely, Fritz, *Lost Sea of the Exodus* (2016), 61, 217, also makes passing reference to this solution, affirming that Israel traveled "both night and day, likely hurriedly, at least until the destruction of the Egyptian army." Yet even Fritz acknowledges that the first site Israel visited after departing Rameses was Succoth (located by him at Tell el-Maskhuta, just over twenty miles [32 km] from Rameses). The text informs us that Israel paused to "make camp" at Succoth (Num 33:5b, √ḥnh) and later "broke camp" at Succoth and reconvened its journey (Exod 13:20a; Num 33:6a, √nsʿ), and where, it must be added, the Israelites even spent time building fires and baking bread (Exod 12:39). Of course all of these events at nearby Succoth took place prior to the demise of the Egyptian army.

52. In contrast to the rather breakneck pace of travel across the Sinai proposed by Garrett and others, the text that supplies the fullest elaboration on the relationship between the movement of the pillar of cloud and the pillar of fire, and the movement of Israel "setting up camp" and "setting out from camp" (Num 9:15–23; note the same itinerary lexicography as listed above), outlines a more modest pace. That narrative describes remaining at a campsite "until morning" or for "two days," or "a few days," or "many days," or "a month, or even a longer time." Whereas the immediate context of this text relates to the establishment of the tabernacle, which occurred after Israel had arrived at Mt. Sinai, it is significant that Neh 9:9–15 rehearses this same reality in a context that also relates to events that preceded their arrival at the mountain of God. This information can also help explain why, e.g., some thirty days are said to have lapsed between the day Israel departed Rameses (Num 33:3, "fifteenth day of the first month") and the day Israel arrived at the "wilderness [*midbār*] of Sin" (Exod 16:1, "fifteenth day of the second month"), and yet only seven to eight intermediate campsites have been recorded in the text (see table 2).

TABLE 2: Earliest campsites in Israel's exodus from Egypt

Day of travel	Narrative account (Exod 12:37–17:1)	Itinerary account (Num 33:1–12a)	Notation of making camp ($\sqrt{hnh}$)	Notation of breaking camp ($\sqrt{ns^c}$)
Day 1 (i.e., the nighttime that followed the Passover)[53]	Rameses to Succoth (12:37)	Rameses to Succoth (33:5)	Num 33:5b	Exod 13:20a; Num 33:6a
Day 2	Succoth to Etham, on the edge of the *midbār* (13:20)	Succoth to Etham, on the edge of the *midbār* (33:6)	Exod 13:20b; Num 33:6b	Num 33:7a
Day 3	Etham to Pi-hahiroth, between Migdol and the *yām*, in front of Baal-zephon, beside the *yām* (14:2; cf. 14:9b)	Etham to Pi-hahiroth, near Baal-zephon, beside Migdol (33:7)	Exod 14:2ab, 9; Num 33:7b	Num 33:8a

---

53. Israel's Passover occurred on the fourteenth day of the first month (Exod 12:6; cf. Lev 23:5; Num 28:16; Josh 5:10; Ezra 6:19; Ezek 45:21). Since a "day" in Israel was measured from sunset to sunset (e.g., Gen 1:5; Exod 12:18; Lev 11:24; 15:5–7; 23:32; Deut 23:11; Neh 13:19; Ps 55:17 [MT 55:18]; cf. Luke 23:54; 2 Cor 11:25), Israel's departure in the nighttime that followed the Passover would be demarcated as the fifteenth day of the first month (see Num 33:3), see Levine, *Numbers 21–36*, 515.

Day of travel	Narrative account (Exod 12:37–17:1)	Itinerary account (Num 33:1–12a)	Notation of making camp ($\sqrt{hnh}$)	Notation of breaking camp ($\sqrt{ns^c}$)
Day 4 (i.e., the night-time that followed day 3)	Moses stretched out his hand over the sea and the water was divided (14:21; cf. Isa 10:26b); Israel went into the middle of the sea [*bətôk hayyām*] on dry ground [*bayyabbāšâ*] (14:22, 16b, 29; 15:19b; cf. Josh 4:22b; Heb 11:29a); the Egyptians went into the middle of the sea [*el-tôk hayyām*] (14:23) and were drowned (14:28b; cf. 15:1–21; Neh 9:11; Ps 78:13; 136:15; Heb 11:29b); Moses then set out from *yam sûf* and entered the *midbār* (15:22; cf. 15:4b; Ps 106:9)	Israel passed through the middle of the sea [*bətôk hayyām*] and then entered the *midbār* (33:8)		
Day 5	First of three days traversing the *midbār* of Shur (15:22b)	First of three days traversing the *midbār* of Etham (33:8b)		
Day 6	Second of three days traversing the *midbār* of Shur	Second of three days traversing the *midbār* of Etham		
Day 7	Third of three days traversing the *midbār* of Shur, to Marah (15:22b–23)	Third of three days traversing the *midbār* of Etham, to Marah (33:8c)	Num 33:8c	Num 33:9a

Day of travel	Narrative account (Exod 12:37–17:1)	Itinerary account (Num 33:1–12a)	Notation of making camp (√ḥnh)	Notation of breaking camp (√nsʿ)
Day 8	Marah to Elim (15:27)	Marah to Elim (33:9)	Exod 15:27b; Num 33:9b	Exod 16:1a; Num 33:10a
Day 9		Elim to yam sûf [54] (33:10)	Num 33:10b	Num 33:11a
Day 10	To the midbār of Sin [śîn] (16:1b)	To the midbār of Sin [śîn] (33:11b)	Num 33:11b	Num 33:12a

The necessity of nocturnal illumination is very much a central part of the earliest stages of the exodus narrative. Thus, for example, we learn that Israel's initial leg in its journey—from Rameses to Succoth—began in the middle of the night. In this regard, one notes that the firstborn in the land died *at midnight* (Exod 12:29; cf. 11:4; 12:12); the pharaoh, his officials, and all the Egyptians arose *in the night* (12:30); the king summoned Moses and Aaron *during the night* and told them to be gone (12:31). In the same manner, the Egyptians *were urgent* with the people of Israel, and they sent them out *immediately*, even before their bread was leavened (12:33–34). We are told Israel was *thrust out* of Egypt and *did not tarry* (12:39b; cf. Ps 105:38). Finally, Scripture

---

54. In any scenario, this is not the same location as the exodus miracle, also identified as *yam sûf* (see the "day 4" entry in table 2). Assuming Israel's initial destination after its deliverance was somewhere in the rugged granite high plateau of the southern Sinai Peninsula, and assuming the miracle had taken place either at one of the smaller inland lakes adjacent to the delta or at the northernmost portion of the Gulf of Suez, the most convenient and natural route south would have been to hug the comparatively flat and open coastal plain abutting the eastern shore of the Gulf of Suez, perhaps as far south as Wadi Feiran, which would have provided direct access to the oasis at Feiran, the most prolific water supply in the western Sinai (see *TBA*, "Sinai, Archaeology and History" map, following map B/X/12; and see the modern road). Camping near the gulf at any place along that stretch of plain could be expected to have been identified *as yam sûf*.

records that in the same way this was *a night* of vigil, so *this same night* [of Passover] will be *a night* of vigil [in Passovers to come] (12:42; cf. Deut 16:1b). Accordingly, the Israelites surely required nocturnal illumination as they were departing Rameses.

Similarly, the exodus event itself took place during the nighttime, presumably in the span of about eight hours or less. First in this regard, we are told that the Egyptian army was bearing down on the Israelites *as night fell* (Exod 14:9, 20a), but yet the Egyptians did not come near the Israelites *all night long* (14:20b). At some point, Moses raised his rod over the *yām*, causing a strong east wind to divide the water, and thus enabling the Israelites safe passage *all through the night* (14:21–22; cf. 15:8, 10). Then *in the morning watch* (i.e., the final night watch, which ended as the morning rays of dawn would begin to appear [1 Sam 11:11; cf. Judg 7:19; Lam 2:19]),[55] the Egyptian chariots began to get clogged in the mire (14:23–25); and finally *at sunrise* the flooding waters drowned the Egyptians in the *yām* (14:26–28). Thus at a second critical moment early in their exodus pilgrimage, the Israelites doubtless required illumination at night for safe travel.

Beyond those two historical incidents, however, there is little indication that Israel traveled at night. To the contrary, their itinerary texts are filled with a long series of place names identifying sites where they stopped at night and made camp along their journey. They could have engaged in other night travel, of course, but the text does not indicate that they did so with any regularity. Several texts relating to nighttime activities during Israel's forty years in the wilderness appear to presuppose something that took place in the camp, not on the march (e.g., Exod 16:13; 40:38; Num 11:9; 14:1; Deut 1:33; cf. Ps 105:39).

Nevertheless, nocturnal illumination under ordinary circumstances was still vitally imperative for a people on the move, in order to enable the Israelites to care for normal personal needs (food, water), for their families, for their flocks and herds, and for requisite hygenic and societal functions overnight. Camped successively as they would

---

55. See, e.g., Dozeman, *Commentary on Exodus*, 499.

have been in a very remote, harsh, rugged, uneven, and sometimes boulder-strewn wilderness terrain, and surrounded by deadly creatures of the night (e.g. Num 21:6–9; Deut 8:15, venomous snakes [*nāḥāš śārāph*] and scorpions ['*aqrāb*]), Israel *routinely* stood in need of nocturnal illumination, far beyond the dim lunar reflections that might occasionally have been available on a clear night. In particular, several species of scorpions are known to have inhabited the Sinai and the Great Syrian Desert, including some of the most dangerous and lethal species in the world.[56] Anyone who has spent even four nights camping in the interior of either of these two deserts (not to mention four decades)—where the surrounding darkness at night is stark and utterly palpable—is fully aware of the recklessness of moving only ten feet [3 m] from one's sleeping bag, without first having in hand a light. Absent these modern inventions, the Israelites stood very much in need of nocturnal illumination for nighttime activities and safe passage inside and around their camp, routinely and benevolently supplied by the Lord through the pillar of fire.[57]

2.3 A SEQUENCE OF EGYPT, *YAM SÛF*, WILDERNESS, SINAI

I should also indicate what I perceive to be a faulty and/or inconsistent sequence in the geographic scheme of Fritz. The biblical record provides the following sequence relating to Israel's deliverance at *yam sûf*: (1) the people of Israel set out from Egypt (e.g., Exod 12:41b;

---

56. Consult, e.g., B. C. Birch, "Scorpion," *ISBE* 4:357–58; *HALOT*, 875. Refer also to Mohamed A. A Omran and Alistar McVean, "Intraspecific Variation in Scorpion *LEIURUS QUINQUESTRIATUS* Venom Collected from Egypt (Sinai and Aswan Deserts)," *Journal of Toxicology: Toxin Reviews* 18 (2000), 247–64; see also Adrienne Mayor, "Scorpions in Antiquity," *Wonders and Marvels*, http://www.wondersandmarvels.com/2013/12/scorpions-in-antiquity.html. For a convenient overview with pictures, see *Wikipedia*, s.v. "Deathstalker," last modified April 24, 2020, 19:23; https://en.wikipedia.org/wiki/Deathstalker.

57. While oil lamps antedated the exodus events by a considerable margin of time, it is unlikely that a steady supply of oil would have been available in the desert, where olive trees do not grow naturally in numbers. Biblical references to oil lamps during Israel's forty years of wandering appear to relate to their use in the tabernacle (e.g., Exod 25:37; 40:24–25; Lev 24:2–4; Num 4:9; 8:2–3), not in daily private use.

Num 33:1); (2) they then encounter *yam sûf* (e.g., Exod 14:2); (3) this
is followed immediately by their entry into "wilderness" (e.g., Exod
15:22, the wilderness of Shur; Num 33:8, the wilderness of Etham
[see above, §2.2; see below, §2.4]); and eventually (4) they arrive
at the wilderness of Sinai (e.g., Exod 19:1b; Num 33:15) (see map 2).

On the one hand, if according to the view of Fritz, *yam sûf* must
be equated with the Gulf of Aqaba/Elat, one would then be obliged
in theory to argue that traversing the rugged intermediate terrain
across the entire Sinai Peninsula, from the Egyptian site of Succoth
across to the Gulf of Aqaba/Elat, a distance in excess of two hundred
land miles (322 km), has been completely omitted from the biblical
record in both literary accounts. This is not merely a case of selective reference to possible successive campsites; rather, this requires
that the entirety of the Sinai has been completely omitted from both
of the biblical records. If, on the other hand, Fritz wishes somewhat
arbitrarily to locate the site of Etham and the wilderness of Etham
near modern Wadi Girafi,[58] some twenty miles (32 km) west of the

---

58. Fritz, *Lost Sea of Exodus* (2016), 220–34; figs. 14.7; 14.13; 14.15; and 14.17. He makes this
otherwise unfounded assertion based on what he considers to be two linguistic clues. His first
clue is a Gesenius's citation ("1979, 864"), which is said to reference a "Coptic Egyptian" word,
meaning "boundary of the sea" (Fritz, *Lost Sea of Exodus* [2016], 220). When one turns to the
referenced page in Gesenius's *Hebrew and Chaldee Lexicon*, the entries found there begin with
the Hebrew letter *tsade* (צ), not *aleph* (א, i.e., the first Hebrew letter of the word Etham), and
no entry on that page is found to have such a meaning. On the other hand, the entry for Etham
found in Gesenius reads: "Etham, possibly a fort" (Gesenius, *Hebrew and Chaldee Lexicon*, 87
[which is said to link to Strong's entry #864, which may provide the bibliographic source of
Fritz's mistaken citation]; and see the entry in BDB, 87, "Etham: in Egypt, a place on [the] edge
of desert" [with accompanying biblical citations]). Fritz's second source is a British traveler,
Richard F. Burton, "Itineraries of the Second Khedivial Expedition: Memoir Explaining the
New Map of Midian Made by the Egyptian Staff-Officers," *Journal of the Royal Geographical
Society of London* 49 (1879): 44–45, who in the referenced passage is actually discussing various
geographical nomenclature in the Arabian Hejaz, a region of western Saudi Arabia aligning
the *east* coast of the Red Sea and the Gulf of Aqaba/Elat. This portion of Burton's text has
nothing to do with the Sinai, and thus this reference has no direct bearing in the context of
Fritz's discussion of biblical Etham at Wadi Girafi. A similar pattern appears in the itineration
of Garrett who argues that Israel journeys from Succoth (= Tell el-Maskhuta, in the land of
Goshen) to Etham (for him, the northern tip of the Gulf of Aqaba/Elat, *à la* Humphreys; see
below page 58, note 85), thereby as a consequence omitting the entire Sinai Peninsula in both
biblical narratives (Garrett, *Commentary on Exodus*, 384). In fact Garrett argues that Israel
traveled continuously, both day and night with no intermediate encampments, between Succoth
and the Gulf of Aqaba/Elat.

Gulf of Aqaba/Elat and more than sixty-five miles (105 km) from the site of Nuweiba, his preferred point of the miraculous water crossing, this then necessitates locating the site of Etham and the "wilderness of Etham" *west* of the Gulf of Aqaba/Elat (and note his western placement of both the site and the wilderness on maps 14.13 and 14.15), whereas the biblical account is unambiguously clear that Israel sequentially encountered "the wilderness of Etham" only *after* passing through *yam sûf* (Num 33:8ab) (see below §2.4).[59]

2.4 THE LOCATION OF SHUR AND
THE WILDERNESS OF SHUR

We are told in the book of Numbers that upon being delivered at *yam sûf*, Israel continued their journey in the wilderness of Etham before the people came to the site of Marah (33:8), but in the account of the book of Exodus, the children of Israel are said to have begun their journey from *yam sûf* in the wilderness of Shur before coming to the site of Marah (15:22). Unlike a lack of geographic clarity that exists for Etham and the wilderness of Etham, we have relatively lucid, revealing geographic indicators for the location of Shur and the wilderness of Shur (see above, ch. 1). In this regard, we learn that Abraham is said to have journeyed, presumably from Mamre/Hebron (Gen 18:1; 20:1), toward the Negeb (*'arṣāh hannegeb*[60]), where the patriarch "took up residence in Gerar,"[61] said in the text to have been "located between Kadesh[-barnea = 'Ain el-Qudeirat] and Shur" (Gen 20:1). The location of Mamre, biblical Negeb, Kadesh-barnea, and Gerar are all known with near certainty, so this means Abraham took up

---

59. Somewhat as an aside, to hold that the exodus event took place at some point in the Gulf of Aqaba/Elat requires the presumption that direct Egyptian military/political control extended at that time throughout the whole of the Sinai Peninsula, which on current evidence is an extremely difficult historical case to attempt to make, east of Serabit el-Khadim with its rich mineral resources, and especially in the southeast quadrant of the peninsula. Fritz and others leave this dilemma largely unaddressed.

60. As over against the modern Negev, the biblical Negeb is restricted largely to the Arad-Beersheba alluvial basin and westward into the open bay of Gerar (cf. *TBA* B/IV/5).

61. Gerar is identified as Tel Haror, some fourteen miles (22.5 km) southeast of Gaza; see its placement in *MAB*, 103, map 31, and on the Madaba mosaic map; cf. page 55, note 76 below.

residence in a territory located in extreme southwest Canaan and near southernmost Philistia. And since Gerar is said to have been located "between Kadesh-barnea [to the southeast of Tel Haror] and Shur" (*bên-qādēš ûbên-šûr*), this demands that from ʿAin el-Qudeirat, Shur has to be situated in a westward direction beyond Tel Haror and at a place through which a road passed (Gen 16:7, *derek šûr*). Accordingly, this text suggests Shur and the wilderness of Shur should be sought in the northernmost stretches of the Sinai, from Kadesh-barnea and Gerar in the direction of Egypt.

This initial observation is strongly reinforced by two additional clarifying texts, in which we are told that Shur was situated "in close proximity to Egypt" (Gen 25:18; 1 Sam 15:7). These two texts employ identical phraseology: *šûr ʾăšer ʿal-pənê miṣrayim* ("Shur, which is in close proximity to Egypt," cf. Josephus, *Ant.* 6.140). I focus here in particular on the prepositional phrase *ʿal-pənê*, which literally means "before the face/presence of; beside/near; in the front of; in the sight of; on the surface/face of."[62]

More to the point, the prepositional expression *ʿal-pənê* occurs nearly twenty times in the Old Testament in an explicitly geographical context (i.e., geographical entity A is *ʿal-pənê* geographical entity B), meaning without exception "near, opposite, facing, beside, adjacent," or some such proximate designation:

- Gen 23:19; 25:9; 49:30; 50:13—The field of Machpelah is *ʿal-pənê* Mamre/Hebron.

- Num 21:11—Iye-abarim is *ʿal-pənê* Moab (cf. Num 33:44).

- Num 21:20—The overlooking summit of Mt. Pisgah is *ʿal-pənê* the Jeshimon (in context, this is the desert wasteland situated immediately east of the Dead Sea).[63]

---

62. BDB, 818; *HALOT*, 943–44; *DCH* 6:720; e.g., Exod 33:19; 34:6; Lev 16:14; Num 12:3; Deut 14:2; 2 Sam 14:7b; 1 Kgs 18:1; Isa 23:17; Jer 16:4.

63. See LaMoine F. DeVries, "Jeshimon," *ABD* 3:769; J. F. Prewett, "Jeshimon," *ISBE* 2:1032.

- Num 23:28—The overlooking summit of Mt. Peor is ʿal-pǝnê the Jeshimon.

- Num 33:7b—Pi-hahiroth is ʿal-pǝnê Baal-zephon.

- Deut 32:49—Mt. Nebo is ʿal-pǝnê Jericho (see also 34:1).

- Josh 13:3—Shihor is ʿal-pǝnê Egypt (Egyptian š-ḥr, meaning "waters of Horus," is situated adjacent to the eastern delta).[64]

- Josh 13:25—Aroer is ʿal-pǝnê Rabbah/Amman (context requires this to be the "Gadite Aroer," possibly Tell el-Umeire, not the "Reubenite Aroer" [e.g., Josh 13:16]).

- Josh 15:8—The boundary of Jebus/Jerusalem is ʿal-pǝnê the Hinnom Valley.

- Josh 17:7—Michmethah is ʿal-pǝnê Shechem.

- Josh 19:11—The Kishon River is ʿal-pǝnê Jokneam.

- 1 Kgs 17:3, 5—The Kerith stream is ʿal-pǝnê the Jordan River.

- 2 Kgs 23:12–13—The Kidron Valley is ʿal-pǝnê Jerusalem.

- Zech 14:4—The Mount of Olives is ʿal-pǝnê Jerusalem.[65]

I have uncovered no unambiguous exceptions to this syntactical or geographical reality found embedded in such a construction.

The same phraseology is also employed in other kinds of geographical settings where the presence of ʿal-pǝnê likewise demands

---

64. Cf. Manfred Bietak, "Comments on the Exodus," in *Egypt, Israel, Sinai: Archaeological and Historical Relationships in the Biblical Period*, ed. Anson F. Rainey (Tel Aviv: Tel Aviv University, 1987), 165–66; Rainey and Notley, *Sacred Bridge*, 118–20.

65. Theoretically the close proximity could lie toward any one of the four cardinal compass points; thus, e.g., it might lie to the south (e.g. Josh 18:5), to the west (e.g. Josh 15:8), or to the east (e.g. Deut 32:49; Zech 14:4). Whatever the direction, it is rather the obvious denotation of *close geographic proximity* being emphasized with the use of the prepositional phrase.

close proximity. Thus, for example, when told that David was hiding from him at En-gedi, Saul immediately marched with his men in pursuit of David ʿal-pənê the Crags of the Wild Goats, where the two men came into direct physical contact (1 Sam 24:2 [MT 24:3]). In similar fashion, as they were in pursuit of Abner, Joab and Abishai are said to have come to the hill of Ammah ʿal-pənê Giah, on the way to Gibeon (2 Sam 2:24). In Isaiah 18:2, watercraft vessels are ʿal-pənê the Nile, and in Ezekiel 37:2, Ezekiel was taken ʿal-pənê a valley filled with many bones. In all of these cases, where the locations of both geographical entities A and B are known or can be reasonably inferred, they are without exception situated in close spatial proximity to one another, oftentimes within visual proximity. Moreover, one further notes this eloquent geographical usage of ʿal-pənê in the immediate context of Genesis 25:18 (and see 25:9b).

Accordingly the clause šûr ʾăšer ʿal-pənê miṣrayim (Gen 25:18; 1 Sam 15:7) plainly designates a close geographic proximity to Egypt. That is to say, "Shur is ʿal-pənê Egypt." Despite this, Fritz offers this bold declaration, "The statement that *Shur* 'faced' Egypt does not require any certain proximity."[66] He argues this without offering so much as a syllable of evidentiary support. To locate the site of Shur and the wilderness of Shur in the Transjordanian mountains of Edom, more than two hundred roadway miles (322 km) from the eastern edge of Egypt,[67] or to argue that ʿal-pənê in these two texts merely denotes the latitude of Shur, not the location, and to situate Shur in faraway Arabah[68]—without offering collateral evidence of any sort— is in my view an extraordinarily glaring violation of Hebrew lexicography and grammar and a strained and unsustainable assertion with respect to Hebrew syntax. In the case of Garrett, it would also be an extremely odd way (unprecedented and anachronistic) of expressing geographic intent in a preclassical world, before the concept of latitude/longitude was introduced into geographical consciousness

---

66. Fritz, *Lost Sea of Exodus* (2016), 282.

67. Fritz, *Lost Sea of Exodus* (2016), 282–89.

68. So Garrett, *Commentary on Exodus*, 415–17.

and mapmaking. Given the strength and consistency of the relevant evidence, I conclude that use of the prepositional phrase ʿal-pənê *demands* that the site of Shur and the wilderness of Shur must be sought in close geographical proximity to Egypt (see map 2).[69]

It may also be significant that the Hebrew word *šûr* occurs several times as a common noun, normally translated "wall(s)."[70] The possible relevance of this comment concerns a Middle Egyptian text that describes a palace servant named Sinuhe, who fled for his life from Egypt to Canaan.[71] Sinuhe is said to have set out from the vicinity of Giza, crossed over the Nile River and come to the Red Mountain (Jebel al-Ahmar). From that point he turned in a northerly direction and reached "the Walls of the Ruler," which the text goes

---

69. The text of Gen 25:18 adds an additional qualification: Shur is ʿal-pənê Egypt bōʾăkâ ʾaššûrāh ("in going to/as one goes to Asshur"). What "Asshur" means here is by no means clear. The term has been understood to refer to a clan/tribe inhabiting Sinai, mentioned earlier in this same chapter (25:3; cf. Gen 10:22; so S. R. Driver, *The Book of Genesis* [London: Methuen, 1911], 243; E. A. Speiser, *Genesis*, AB 1 [New York: Doubleday, 1964], 188; Gordon J. Wenham, *Genesis 16–50*, WBC 2 [Dallas: Word, 1994], 165; Kenneth Mathews, *Genesis 11:27–50:26*, NAC 1B [Nashville: Broadman & Holman, 2005], 363). Alternatively, the term has also been construed as an (anachronistic) reference to the Iron Age nation of Assyria. With either of these interpretations, however, commentators likewise continue to situate Shur in very close proximity to Egypt, on the east side (see, e.g., Franz Delitzsch, *A New Commentary on Genesis* [Edinburgh: T&T Clark, 1899], 128; G. Charles Aalders, *Genesis* [Grand Rapids: Zondervan, 1981], 2:77; Claus Westermann, *Genesis 12–36*, CC [Minneapolis: Fortress, 1995], 399; Victor Hamilton, *The Book of Genesis: Chapters 18–50*, NICOT [Grand Rapids: Eerdmans, 1995], 169; S. R. Driver, *Notes on the Hebrew Text and the Topography of the Books of Samuel*, 2nd ed. [Oxford: Clarendon, 1913], 123; Peter Ackroyd, *The First Book of Samuel*, CBC [Cambridge: Cambridge University Press, 1971], 121; P. Kyle McCarter, *1 Samuel*, AB 8 [New York: Doubleday, 1980], 262, 266; Joyce Baldwin, *1 and 2 Samuel*, TOTC [Downers Grove, IL: InterVarsity Press, 1988], 114; Robert Gordon, *1 & 2 Samuel* [Exeter: Paternoster, 1986], 143; David Tsumura, *The First Book of Samuel*, NICOT [Grand Rapids: Eerdmans, 2007], 394; Ralph W. Klein, *1 Samuel*, WBC 10 [Nashville: Nelson, 2008], 144, 150; and A. Graeme Auld, *I & II Samuel: A Commentary*, OTL [Louisville: Westminster John Knox, 2011], 168). In an effort to reinforce his contention that Shur must be situated in the Arabah, Garrett curiously translates this text as follows: "Shur is opposite Egypt as one goes [from Havilah] to Assyria" (Garrett, *Commentary on Exodus*, 417). It is easy to see how such an understanding has failed to gain scholarly traction, either geographically or syntactically: the land of Havilah (whether located in the Arabian Peninsula or in Africa in the vicinity of modern Ethiopia) can hardly be said to be ʿal-pənê Egypt, nor does it figure into the immediate syntax of the demonstrative clause that follows "Shur" (and notice that Garrett is obliged to place his syntactically unfounded insertion inside brackets).

70. BDB, 1004; *HALOT*, 1453; see Gen 49:22b; 2 Sam 22:30b//Ps 18:30b; Ezra 4:12–13, 16; so NIV, ESV, NLT, NRSV.

71. See *ANET*, 19; *COS* 1.38.77–78; *AEL* 1:222–35.

on to declare were constructed "to repel the Asiatics and to crush the Sand Dwellers." Apparently set up as a physical deterrent to the unwanted influx of peoples located adjacent to Egypt's east, Sinuhe's walls may be a reference to the north-south series of Egyptian fortresses that line the eastern delta between the Mediterranean Sea and the Gulf of Suez,[72] and/or to the defensive canal that connected the Mediterranean with places as far south as Timsah Lake, and which also served as a military deterrent.[73] In either event, one again distinctively has in view the terrain *adjacent* to Egypt on the eastern front.[74]

2.5 THE LOCATION OF THE BIBLICAL EXODUS IN EARLY TRADITIONS

Evidence from early Jewish or Christian traditions relating to the location of a particular biblical event should normally be given consideration in the context of other lines of reasoning. Whether and when early traditions should be considered primary or secondary evidence continues understandably to be debated in scholarly circles, but in principle I would contend that traditions do constitute *evidence* of some sort and should not de facto be ruled out of evidentiary bounds. Perhaps a given tradition can be reinforced with another form of evidence, or perhaps it cannot. But in either event, early traditions as a category should not be summarily dismissed in an a priori manner. The many publications of John Wilkinson are widely recognized as some of the most comprehensive and authoritative resources relating to early Christian traditions, and I should imagine, as a result, his studied, nuanced judgments on the question of the reliability of early

---

72. See §2.2 above; cf. David R. Seely, "Shur, Wilderness of," *ABD* 5:1230.

73. See *MAB*, map 33.

74. A Middle Kingdom wall or a chain of fortifications that stretched from Pelusium to Heliopolis, constructed by Pharaoh Sesostris (III?) to protect Egypt against unwanted incursions from the east, is later described by Diodorus (1.57.4); see also Kitchen, *Reliability of the Old Testament*, 259–60. At present there is no way of knowing for certain if either Sinuhe's wall or Sesostris' wall are in any way related to each other or whether either can be related to the biblical Shur/wall, but that possibility cannot be ruled out.

FIGURE 5: **Timsah Lake**

The biblical roadway "the way to Shur" (Gen 16:7) extended eastward from the Nile Delta through the Wadi Tumilat, past the biblical sites of Pithom/Tell er-Retaba and Succoth/Tell el-Maskhuta, to a point near Timsah Lake (pictured here), one of the inland lakes along the eastern edge of Egypt, between the Mediterranean Sea and the Gulf of Suez, thought perhaps to have been biblical *yam sûf*. Buildings in the background and on the horizon of the image are part of the modern Egyptian city of Ismalia. (Photo by Banja-Frans Mulder, via Wikimedia Commons, under CC BY 3.0)

traditions—especially relating to the earliest portions of the Byzantine period—merit special attention.[75]

In the case of the location of the exodus event at *yam sûf* in particular, beyond the translational understanding of the LXX Jewish scholars, Jewish tradition as we saw above can be traced back to the first Christian century and the writings of Josephus (*Ant.* 2.315), who, when speaking of the Israelite departure from Egypt, indicated Israel had arrived at the site of Baal-zephon, *beside erythra thalassa*,

---

75. E.g., John Wilkinson, "Christian Pilgrims in Jerusalem during the Byzantine Period," *PEQ* 108 (1976): 75–101; Wilkinson, *Jerusalem Pilgrims before the Crusades* (Warminster: Aris & Phillips, 1977), 37–39; Wilkinson, "Jewish Holy Places and the Origins of Christian Pilgrimage," in *The Blessings of Pilgrimage*, ed. Robert Ousterhout (Urbana: University of Illinois Press, 1990), 41–53, and see the additional bibliographic sources cited there.

on the third day. And it was from that locality that the exodus subsequently occurred (2.334–38). Christian tradition begins to emerge in the fourth century, in the near aftermath of Constantine's decision to end the persecution of Christians and to make Christianity a force within the Roman Empire. Whatever the emperor's motivation(s) may have been, this decision had a dramatic impact on early Byzantine Christianity, including in the realm of early Christian pilgrimage. Thus, as early as c. AD 382, more than one hundred and fifty years before the emperor Justinian erected St. Catherine's Monastery at the foot of Jebel Musa, a mountain in the southern Sinai Peninsula commonly identified as the location of biblical Mt. Sinai, the early pilgrim Egeria visited an exodus crossing site in close proximity to Egypt, along the isthmus of land separating the Mediterranean Sea and the Gulf of Suez.[76] This same tradition persisted for a long while, as documented in the early Christian writings of Cosmas Indicopleustes, a devout Greek merchant (c. AD 550);[77] the Piacenza pilgrim (c. AD 570);[78] Dicuil, an Irish monk and geographer (c. AD 765);[79] the saintly

76. John Wilkinson, *Egeria's Travels to the Holy Land*, 3rd ed. (Warminster: Aris & Phillips, 1999), 94–95 and map, 101–118, esp. 101–4 [Y4–10]; see also Daniel F. Caner, *History and Hagiography from the Late Antique Sinai* (Liverpool: Liverpool University Press, 2010), 212–14, 227. The "Madaba Map," a large multicolored mosaic map, the vestige of which covers most of the floor of the St. George Greek Orthodox Church in the Jordanian town of Madaba/Medeba (about twenty miles [32 km] southwest of Amman), dates to the early sixth century and is the earliest known original depiction of biblical events in the Holy Land. The map portrays the land mass between Byblos and Damascus in the north, as far south as the Nile Delta, and from the Mediterranean shoreline as far east as the land of Moab. While a Red Sea crossing point does not appear, in the somewhat obliterated southwest corner of the map, various distributaries of the Nile are depicted and named, including the easternmost Pelusiac branch, as well as a number of eastern towns, e.g., Tanis, Sais, Hermopolis, and Pelusium. Just east of the delta, the mosaic displays the site of "Rephidim, where Amalek fought against Israel" (see Exod 17:8–16) and the "wilderness of Sin [*Erēmos Sin*], where manna and quails were sent down" (see Exod 16:1–36; Num 11:4–35). Unfortunately, nothing farther east in the Sinai appears in the remains of the mosaic (see Michael Avi-Yonah, *The Madaba Mosaic Map* [Jerusalem: Israel Exploration Society, 1954], pls. 5, 10; Herbert Donner, *The Mosaic Map of Madaba* [Kampen: Kok Pharos, 1992], ##97, 98, 130, 134, 138).

77. Wilkinson, *Jerusalem Pilgrims*, 122–123; Caner, *History and Hagiography*, 248.

78. Wilkinson, *Jerusalem Pilgrims*, 148–49; Caner, *History and Hagiography*, 261.

79. Wilkinson, *Jerusalem Pilgrims*, 231–32.

Epiphanius (date uncertain, but not prior to the seventh century);[80] Bernard the monk (c. AD 870);[81] and others who came later to commemorate the place of the miraculous crossing. So far as I am able to discern, early Jewish and Christian traditions relating to the exodus event are locationally consistent, placing the event in very close proximity to Egypt.

Concerning early traditions identifying modern Jebel Musa as biblical Mt. Sinai, several scholars, including Fritz,[82] argue that not being able to trace back the antiquity earlier than the third or fourth centuries AD—more than twelve hundred years after the biblical events were originally written—effectively invalidates the tradition. I offer this response. As anyone who works on the historical geography of the Bible well knows, if such a chronologically disjunctive criterion were to be applied to the wide majority of events recorded in the Bible, this same disqualification would have to obtain. For the simple fact is we do not have evidence of earlier traditions or antiquarian research relating to the location of most biblical events prior to this time, and in some cases not until an even later era.

Before that time, efforts to discover the location of a biblical event either were never recorded in documentary form that has survived or—especially for locations involving events which had transpired at distant and faraway places from Palestine and thus were more difficult to access, such as the locations of the exodus or Mt. Sinai (e.g., Mt. Ararat, Ur of the Chaldeans, Babylon, Harran, Sheba, Tarshish, Thebes, Susa, Nineveh, Gog and Magog)—interest did not exist on any scale and/or travel to such distant and remote points was infeasible for a variety of compelling reasons.[83] Even for places situated

---

80. Wilkinson, *Jerusalem Pilgrims*, 211.

81. Wilkinson, *Jerusalem Pilgrims*, 142.

82. Fritz, *Lost Sea of Exodus* (2016), 208–9; see also Kerkeslager, "Jewish Pilgrimage," 208–13; Kerkeslager, "Mt Sinai—in Arabia?," 34–35; Enns, "Exodus Route and Wilderness Itinerary," 277; Garrett, *Commentary on Exodus*, 105.

83. A comment of the Piacenza pilgrim may be relevant in this regard. His group had traveled in the safety of an escorted caravan from Jerusalem through the heart of the Sinai Peninsula to Jebel Musa. When the time came to reverse course and to return to Jerusalem,

FIGURE 6: **St. Catherine's Monastery and Jebel Musa**

St. Catherine's Monastery, erected by the Roman emperor Justinian in the mid-sixth century, stands adjacent to the base of Jebel Musa, the mountain in the background celebrated in Christian tradition as Mt. Sinai since the fourth Christian century. (Photo by J Ansari, via Wikimedia Commons, under CC BY-SA 4.0)

inside or immediately adjacent to Palestine (e.g., Capernaum, Rachel's Tomb, Jacob's Well, Bethany beyond Jordan, Pool of Siloam, Pool of Bethesda, Emmaus), their locations can only be traced back to the third or fourth Christian centuries. As a consequence, this criterion cannot logically be singled out and applied only to something like the location of the exodus event or Mt. Sinai.

Furthermore, I would argue that such a criterion must be applied with equal rigor to any alternative locations proposed for the exodus crossing or for Mt. Sinai. Is Fritz able to produce an earlier tradition of any sort for his own proposal that the exodus occurred at Nuweiba,

---

however, the pilgrim reports that some members of his group could not bear the thought of retracing their steps northward through the rugged and sterile terrain of the Sinai, so they took a more circuitous but less burdensome return journey to the Holy City (Wilkinson, *Jerusalem Pilgrims*, 147). For a helpful presentation of other challenging issues impinging on pilgrimage in the early church, refer to Peter Walker, "Pilgrimage in the Early Church," in *Explorations in a Christian Theology of Pilgrimage*, ed. Craig Bartholomew and Fred Hughes (Burlington, VT: Ashgate, 2004), 73–91.

his preferred site on the Gulf of Aqaba/Elat (see map 3)?[84] Can he or anyone else who wishes to situate the exodus crossing at the Gulf of Aqaba/Elat produce such a supporting tradition at any time in the Byzantine era or even into the Middle Ages? When do we first learn of someone in Judaism or Christianity traveling to the site of Nuweiba, or for that matter to *any* place contiguous to the Gulf of Aqaba, to commemorate Israel's miraculous deliverance at the Red Sea?[85]

So, I conclude this chapter by returning to Fritz's hypothesis one, "The biblical *Yam Suph* is the Gulf of Aqaba." At the end of the day this is an argument relating fundamentally to biblical exegesis and Near Eastern lexicography. I am again reminded of his insistence that this must be an absolute and inviolable hypothesis, and of his observation that any exception in the biblical record means the hypothesis "will be falsified." In my view, the sheer weight and nature of the biblical and documentary evidence presented here renders Fritz's hypothesis one idiosyncratic and latent with the highest level of doubt. Nor do the facts in this matter allow for a response that these lexicographical/exegetical outcomes must be a function of the difference between a traditional and a critical view of canonical compositionalism, as these conclusions are affirmingly embraced by a broad cross section of both historic and contemporary biblical scholarship, within the discipline and across the entire theological spectrum.

---

84. Fritz, *Lost Sea of Exodus* (2016), 186–203.

85. So far as I am aware, an explicit on-site linkage between the Gulf of Aqaba/Elat and the exodus crossing-point was first made in the year 1978 by Ron Wyatt, an amateur explorer who claimed otherwise to have had the extraordinarily good fortune of discovering Noah's ark, the tower of Babel, the biblical ark of the covenant, and the two original stones of the Decalogue. Like Fritz, Wyatt's choice of crossing point is at the oasis of Nuweiba, at a midway point along the western shore of the Gulf (see map 3). Treasure hunters Larry Williams and Robert Cornuke, convinced the Israelites had crossed the Gulf of Aqaba/Elat at its southernmost extremity, at the Straits of Tiran some 70 miles (112 km) south of the Wyatt/Fritz crossing point, explored that location on-site in early 1988 (see Blum, *Gold of Exodus*, 187–201; see map 3). Finally, physicist Colin J. Humphreys maintains the view that Israel crossed slightly north of the current northern coastline of the Gulf, about 65 miles [104.6 km] north of the Wyatt/Fritz site, a location he investigated on-site in the spring of 1999 and then again in 2001 (Humphreys, *Miracles of Exodus*, 181, 224–60). Suffice to say, in all three cases, various kinds of "evidence" of the crossing at each respective location are alleged to have been discovered.

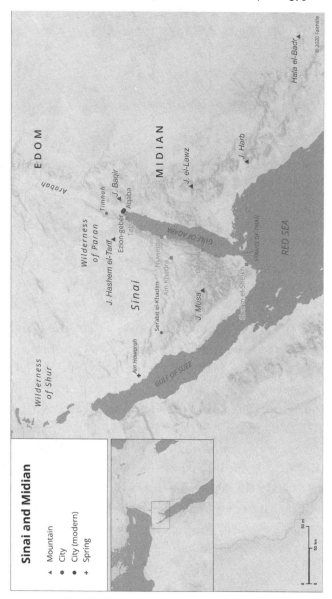

MAP 3: **Sinai and Midian**

Map of the Sinai Peninsula, the Gulf of Aqaba/Elat, and northwestern Saudi Arabia

Chapter 3

EVIDENCE FROM CLASSICAL SOURCES

Now I want to look at the classical Greek and Latin written sources that refer to the *erythra thalassa* or the *mare rubrum*. If Fritz's hypothesis one focuses on written sources found in the Hebrew Bible, his hypothesis two focuses squarely on written Greek and Latin sources that appear in classical literature. In this case, his hypothesis states, "The Gulf of Aqaba has been materially absent from geographical thinking until the modern era."[1] At one point, he elaborates, "The Greek Red Sea concept did not include the Gulf of Aqaba as we know it, because the Greeks were ignorant of its geography."[2] At another, he argues, "The Red Sea was thought to terminate as a single gulf near Egypt during the time of [the translating of] the Septuagint, and for some twenty centuries thereafter."[3] "The ancient Greeks were grossly

---

1. Fritz, "Lost Sea of Exodus" (2006), 12; Fritz, *Lost Sea of Exodus* (2016), 7, 183 (cf. Fritz, "Lost Sea of Exodus" [2006], 73).

2. Fritz, *Lost Sea of Exodus* (2016), xvii; see also Fritz, "Lost Sea of Exodus" (2006), 12.

3. Fritz, *Lost Sea of Exodus* (2016), 107–8; cf. Fritz, "Lost Sea of Exodus" (2006), 81; *Lost Sea of Exodus* (2016), 10, 14, 42, 81, 183.

ignorant of the [Gulf of Aqaba/Elat's] size and position and did not view it as an eastern bifurcation of the Red Sea."[4]

According to this hypothesis, the Gulf of Aqaba/Elat was unknown and unattested in the classical world, was distorted and misshapen as reflected even in various later medieval and Renaissance maps, and the gulf only came to be fully known and explored in the late Renaissance period and into the nineteenth century AD. As a result of its presumed absence throughout the classical period, the Gulf of Aqaba/Elat becomes Fritz's "Lost Sea of the Exodus." Consequently, since in his view the Greek concept of the Red Sea never includes the Gulf of Aqaba/Elat in its purview, and yet according to him the Gulf of Aqaba/Elat is the one and only referent for Hebrew *yam sûf*, Fritz asserts the LXX translators were at a loss to envision the true meaning and location of Hebrew *yam sûf* in Greek, in conjunction with the location of the exodus, and as a result the LXX mistakenly perpetuated faulty Greco-Roman geography in their translation *erythra thalassa*.[5] Therefore, so Fritz contends, the concept of a miraculous Israelite crossing near the eastern edge of Egypt, at the "single gulf near Egypt," followed by a sojourn in the adjacent Sinai Peninsula and at the mountain of Sinai, now erroneously entered the picture of biblical hermeneutics.

---

4. Fritz, *Lost Sea of Exodus* (2016), 44; cf. Fritz, "Lost Sea of Exodus" (2006), 24, 78; Fritz, *Lost Sea of Exodus* (2016), 184.

5. Even theoretically speaking, it is difficult to make a case that anyone living in the twenty-first century, and in a Western cultural milieu—without internal evidence contemporary with the LXX translational undertaking—could fully discern what was in the minds of a group of third century BC Jewish translators in Alexandria, Egypt, when they rendered a certain Hebrew expression "X" with the Greek phrase "Y." And logically speaking, such an assertion can be said to strain credulity when it is extended to what well-educated, competent scholars in antiquity did or did *not* know or understand about an anchor biblical text or how that text was exposited in standard Jewish interpretation among the Jerusalem establishment—again absent internal evidence. Finally, pragmatically speaking, such a judgment borders on the absurd when it is made by anyone in the twenty-first century lacking personal experience having to do with the intricacies of Bible translation and/or appropriate training and pedigree.

3.1 CITATIONAL SOURCES

I wish to offer an evidentiary response on three complementary fronts: (1) classical citational sources, (2) classical exploration sources, and (3) Trajan's construction of the *Via Nova Traiana*. I shall first address some of the citational sources. As early as the sixth century BC, an astonishingly wide array of written sources from the classical period manifests a persistent and enduring awareness of a body of water known as *erythra thalassa//mare rubrum* (or equivalent expressions in Persian or Aramaic; see page 64, note 6)—approximately 825 citations. The writers I reference are hardly a homogeneous lot or share a single worldview or a uniform geographical outlook, even beyond their broad linguistic differentiation. They hail from at least fifteen different countries, ranging from Persia in the east to Algeria and Spain on the western front. Professionally speaking, their ranks include geographers, historians, educators, playwrights, politicians, poets, monarchs, philosophers, clerics, and pilgrims. Religiously, some were Christian and some were Jewish; some adhered to Islam while others presumably followed a form of the Persian, Greek, or Roman state cults. Some wrote for the imperium, while others wrote for the masses. Some seem to have composed with purely historical motivation, others produced propaganda or entertainment, while still others wrote with the pragmatics of transportation or commercial interests in mind. Taken as a whole, this degree of diversity lends credence to the supposition that one is dealing with many discrete, independent empirical witnesses, as they did not all arise from a solitary, common impulse or a single geographical template. Throughout the entirety of the classical era, knowledge of the Red Sea was certainly neither localized nor sectarian.

Even if one assumes that the hundreds of references to *erythra thalassa* or *mare rubrum* found in classical written sources exhibit an essentially historical character or in the main are not mistaken in their geographic details, a great many of them are contextually ambiguous and do not allow for an exact correlation with a modern body of water. The most that can be said of many of these texts is that they tend to

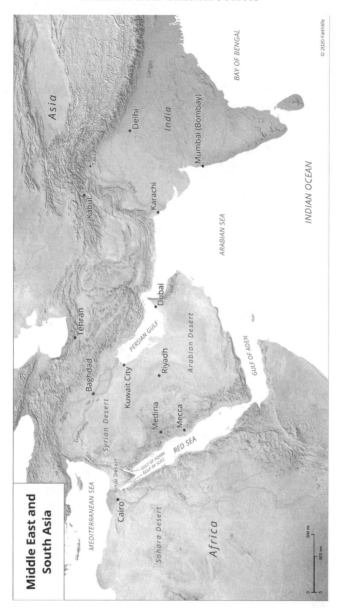

MAP 4: **Middle East and South Asia**

These modern bodies of water were designated as the "Red Sea" in classical literature: the Bay of Bengal, the Indian Ocean, the Persian Gulf, the Gulf of Aden, the modern Red Sea, the Gulf of Suez, and the Gulf of Aqaba/Elat.

designate water located to the south of continental Asia and/or the Arabian subcontinent.[6]

However, a select number of the citations (roughly 115 by my count) are sufficiently precise in their geographic details so as to permit an equation with any one of seven different bodies of water on a modern map: the Bay of Bengal; the Indian Ocean; the Persian Gulf; the Gulf of Aden; the modern Red Sea (i.e., Gulf of Arabia in classical antiquity); the Gulf of Suez; and—most importantly for this essay—the Gulf of Aqaba/Elat (see table 3 and map 4). Table 3 below provides a synopsis of selected classical citations of *erythra thalassa* or *mare rubrum* that can be correlated with a modern body of water.

TABLE 3: Synopsis of selected classical citations of *erythra thalassa* or *mare rubrum*

Location	Citation	Translation / Summary[7]
(1) Bay of Bengal	Philostratus, *Apollonius* 3.50.2	"Apollonius traveled [from the vicinity of Taxila, Pakistan] along the Ganges river for ten days until he reached the coast of *thalattan* ... *Erythran*, the deepest blue sea which gets its name from [king] Erythras, who named the sea after himself." From the Ganges, Apollonius then sailed west and eventually passed the mouth of the Indus river.[8]
(2) Indian Ocean	Xenophon, *Cyropaedia* 8.8.1	"The empire of Cyrus the Great was the greatest and most glorious of all kingdoms of Asia; it was bounded on the east by *Erythra thalattē*, on the north by the Black Sea, on the west by Cyprus and Egypt, and on the south by Ethiopia."

---

6. Such an understanding has long been axiomatic in geographical studies, less so in biblical studies. The myriad of Greek citations are conveniently accessed in the *TLG*, an electronic data bank available through the University of California, Irvine (http://stephanus.tlg.uci.edu/). The many Latin citations may be found in *TLL*, now accessible online via de Gruyter (https://www.degruyter.com/view/db/tll?lang=en). See *TLL* vol. 8, cols. 377–90. Persian literature from the classical period refers to the Red Sea as *drayah* (see Roland G. Kent, *Old Persian: Grammar, Texts, Lexicon*, ed. Murray B. Emeneau and Schuyler Cammann, 2nd ed, rev, American Oriental Series 33 [New Haven: American Oriental Society, 2011], 192), and Aramaic texts denote the body of water as *yammā' śimmōqā'* (see, e.g., 1QapGen [1Q20] 21:17–18).

7. Translations of primary sources are author's own.

8. See also *Periplus of the Erythraean Sea* 63.9–10; Quintus Curtius, *Alexander* 8.9.6.

Location	Citation	Translation / Summary
	Livy, *Epitomes* 42.52.14	"The Roman ancestors subdued all of Europe, crossed into Asia, and with their weapons they opened up a whole world that had been previously unknown even to rumor…. They did not discontinue their conquests until, reaching the barrier of *Rubro mari*, there was nothing left to conquer."[9]
	Eutropius 8.3	"The emperor Trajan conquered Persia, Seleucia, Ctesiphon, Babylon, and Edessiani, and carried everyone before him as far as the coasts of India and *mare Rubrum*."[10]
(3) Persian Gulf	Diodorus 2.11.1–2	"The Tigris and Euphrates rivers [which have their headwaters in the Armenian mountains] enclose Mesopotamia and give this name to the country; after passing through Babylonia, these rivers empty into *Erythran … thalattan*."
	Eusebius, *Onomasticon* 901/164:7–9	"The Tigris river descends [from paradise] to *erythra thalassa*."[11]
	Plutarch, *Lucullus and Cimon* 3.1–2	"[The Roman general] Lucullus crossed the Taurus with his army; he captured and burned all the royal cities of Asia, establishing his territory as far north as Phasis [along the east-central coast of the Black Sea], as far east as Media, and as far south as *erythran thalassan*."
	Arrian, *Anabasis* 7.16.1–2	"[Alexander had discovered that] *ton Persikon* or to use its actual name *Erythran … thalassan*, was only a gulf in the ocean."

---

9. N.B. Livy, *Epitomes* 42.52.15a—*ultimis Indiae oris*—"farthermost shores of India."

10. See also Aristides, *Panathenaic Oration* 119; Valerius Flaccus, *Argonautica* 5.77.

11. In his commentary on Genesis, John Calvin notes the Tigris and Euphrates rivers flow through the garden of Eden and pass into *mare rubrum* (John Calvin, *Ioannis Calvini opera quae supersunt omnia*, vol. 23, Corpus Reformatorum vol. 51, ed. William Baum, Edward Cunitz, and Edward Reuss [Brunsvigae: Schwetschke, 1882], 42).

Location	Citation	Translation / Summary
	Arrian, *Indica* 19.9	"Nearchus [chief of Alexander's naval forces on his eastern campaign] sailed with his fleet from the mouth of the Indus river to *ton kolpon Persikon*, called by some *Erythrēn thalassan.*"
	Androsthenes, via Theophrastus, *Causis Plantarum* 2.5.5	"Tylos [Bahrain] is an island in *Erythran Thalattan.*"[12]
(4) Gulf of Aden	Claudius Ptolemais 6.7.1–2	"Arabia Felix [the southwestern Arabian Peninsula] is terminated on the north by Arabia Petraea, on the northeast by the Persian Gulf ... on the west by the Arabian Gulf, and on the south by *Erythra thalassē.*"[13]
	Herodotus 2.8	Egypt is bounded by the "mountains of Arabia" on the east and by the "rocky mountains" of Libya on the west. With respect to the former, he indicates that the pyramids of Memphis were hewn from quarries in the mountains of Arabia and that their easternmost boundaries yield frankincense (= Somalia). He describes the mountains that stretch on a north-south axis, "extending southward towards a sea called *Erythrēn ... thalassan.*"
(5) Red Sea (classical "Gulf of Arabia")	Quintus Curtius, *Alexander* 4.7.18–19	"Near Ethiopia is an Arabian people known as Trog(l)odytes; their territory extends as far [east] as *Rubrum mare.*"[14]

12. See also Pliny, *Natural History* 12.20.37; Polybius 13.9.2–5 (cf. *BAGRW* map 95 [B4]).

13. In this regard, one should compare Strabo (*Geography* 16.3.1) and Ptolemy; both authors are describing the extent of Arabia Felix, being bordered by the Persian Gulf and the Arabian Gulf, and on the south by *Erythra*; Ptolemy states simply that Arabia Felix was bordered on the south by *Erythra thalassē*, whereas Strabo adds additional clarification: the area was bordered on the south by the great sea that lies outside both gulfs, which as a whole is known as *Erythran*. See also Stephen of Byzantium, *Ethnika* 233.

14. See also Kallimachos, *Regnum Lagidarum* 186.6; Pliny, *Natural History* 2.75.183–184; 13.50.139; Theophrastus, *Plants* 4.7.1; cf. M. Walter Ruppel, *Les Temples Immergés de la Nubie, Der Temple von Dakke*, 3 vols. (Cairo: Institut français d'archéologie orientale, 1930), 3:36 (47a),

Location	Citation	Translation / Summary
(6) Gulf of Suez (Greek: Gulf of Hero-onpolis; Latin: Gulf of Hero-opoliticus)	Herodotus 2.158	Darius I Hystaspes succeeded in completing Necho II's east-west canal through the Wadi Tumilat; this canal was fed by the Nile and took four days to traverse; Herodotus adds, "and it started a little south of Bubastis [T. Basta], went by way of the Arabian town of Patumus [T. er-Retaba/Pithom], and emptied into *Erythrēn thalassan*."[15]

a Ptolemaic text from Nubia that makes mention of collecting taxes from *[e]rythras thalassēs*; Wilhelm Dittenberger, *Orientis Graeci: Inscriptions Selectee*, 2 vols. (Leipzig: Hirzel, 1905), 2:438 (701.9–11 = *Pan Desert* 80), Berenike (Ras Banas) is a city situated on *Erythran thalassan* (cf. Wilfried Van Rengen, "The Written Material from the Graeco-Roman Period," in *Myos Hormos—Quseir al-Qadim*, ed. David Peacock and Lucy Blue, University of Southampton Series in Archaeology 6, BARIS 2286 [Oxford: Archaeopress, 2011], 337, two papyri [probably from Berenike] stating that Berenike is on *erythra thalassē*); Van Rengen, "Written Material," 336, Myos Hormos (Quseir al-Qadim) is (a town situated) on *erythra thalassē*. See also Agatharchides 5.81, 83a; cf. Ross I. Thomas, "Port Communities and the Erythraean Sea Trade," *British Museum Studies in Ancient Egypt and Sudan* 18 (2012): 174.

15. Note as well the boastful claim of Darius himself (*el-Shallûfa Stele*, the find spot was immediately south of the Little Bitter Lake) that he had dug a canal that flows from the Nile as far as *drayah* (= Gulf of Suez, see Pierre Lecoq, *Les inscriptions de la Perse achéménide* [Paris: Gallimard, 1997], 247–48). Darius continues that, as the result of this accomplishment, he was able to issue the order, and ships began navigating the canal and sailing as far as Persia (Pliny, *Natural History* 6.33.165); Ptolemy II Philadelphus (*Pithom Stele*, found at T. el-Maskhuta/Succoth) made a similar claim that he had dug a canal ("the great eastern canal") from the Nile to the "Lake of the Scorpion" (i.e., connecting the Nile with the Red Sea, via the Wadi Tumilat, Timsah Lake, and the Bitter Lakes); cf. Aristotle, *Meteorologica* 1.14.20.

Location	Citation	Translation / Summary
(7) Gulf of Aqaba/ Elat (Greek: Gulf of Aelanites; Latin: Gulf of Aelanit-icus)[16]	Josephus, *Ant.* 8.163	"Solomon constructed many ships in the Egyptian gulf of *Erythras thalassēs* at a place called Ezion-geber, not far from the city of Aila, which is now called Berenike." Josephus adds that Solomon was assisted in this venture by "Eiromos [Hiram] king of Tyre," and that the ships sailed to a place known as Sopheir [Ophir], that now belongs to India.[17]

---

16. This is the entry that directly addresses Fritz's hypothesis two, in which he avers that the Gulf of Aqaba/Elat was not known and never designated by the use of *erythra thalassa* or *mare rubrum* in classical literature. I begin this entry with three texts from Josephus that are geographically eloquent in this regard. Following the Josephus examples, I provide citations of several more classical texts unambiguously referencing the Gulf of Aqaba/Elat as *erythra thalassa//mare rubrum*. For still more relevant citations, refer to Pomponius Mela 3.8.80–81a (see Alain Silberman, *Pomponius Mela, Chorographie*, Collection des Universités de France [Paris: Belles Lettres, 1988], 89–90, 304–8); Agathemerus (see Carolus Müller, *Geographi Graeci Minores*, 2 vols. [Paris: Didot, 1861], 2:475, #14); Pliny, *Natural History* 6.32.143–56, citing one source dating back to c. 100 BC and another which dates to c. 25 BC–AD 24; Lionel Casson, *The Periplus Maris Eruthraei: Text with Introduction, Translation, and Commentary* (Princeton: Princeton University Press, 1989), 61–63, #19a, a source dating to AD 40–70.

17. Cf. 1 Kgs 9:26//2 Chr 8:17–18; note that Fritz repeatedly makes reference to these biblical texts in the context of the location of Ezion-geber, but curiously he makes no mention of this Josephus citation. See Fritz, "Lost Sea of Exodus" (2006), 188; Fritz, *Lost Sea of Exodus* (2016), 93–95. The geographical accuracy of Josephus' declaration is accepted without equivocation by such acclaimed historians as W. W. Tarn, "Ptolemy II and Arabia," *JEA* 15 (1929): 22; M. Rostovtzeff, *The Social & Economic History of the Hellenistic World*, 2nd ed., 2 vols. (Oxford: Clarendon, 1998), 1:387; Michael Avi-Yonah, *The Holy Land from the Persian to the Arab Conquests* (Grand Rapids: Baker, 1966), 41; Victor Tscherikower, *Die hellenistischen Städtegründungen von Alexander dem Grossen bis auf die Römerzeit*, Philologus Supplement 19 (New York: Arno, 1973), 81; Abraham Negev, "The Nabateans and the Provincia Arabia," *ANRW* 2.8:530; Christopher Tuplin, "Darius' Suez Canal and Persian Imperialism," in *Asia Minor and Egypt: Old Cultures in a New Empire; Proceedings of the 1988 Groningen Achaemenid History Workshop*, ed. Heleen Sancisi-Weerdenburg and Amélie Kuhrt, Achaemenid History 6 (Leiden: Nederlands Instituut voor het Nabije Oosten, 1991), 273; Steven Sidebotham, *Berenike and the Ancient Maritime Spice Route* (Berkeley: University of California Press, 2011), 178; David F. Graf, "Map 76 Sinai," *BAGRW* 2:1141; and Getzel M. Cohen, *The Hellenistic Settlements in Syria, the Red Sea Basin, and North Africa* (Berkeley: University of California Press, 2006), 324–25. For Aila/Aqaba = Berenike to the early Ptolemies, see Pomponius Mela 3.80; Tarn, "Ptolemy II and Arabia," 22; Sidebotham, *Berenike*, 178; Cohen, *Hellenistic Settlements*, 324–25.

Location	Citation	Translation / Summary
	Josephus, *Ant.* 9.215–17	In association with his military exploits against the Philistines (including explicit mention of the cities of Gath and Jamnia), against the Arabs, and against the Ammonites, "Ozias [Uzziah] son of Amasias [Amaziah] ... built a city on *Erythras thalassēs* and stationed a garrison there."[18]
	Josephus, *Ant.* 9.243–45	"Arases [Rezin], king of Syria and Damascus, and Phakeas [Pekah], king of Israel, came up against Achaz [Ahaz]; they besieged Jerusalem but they could not conquer the city. However, the king [of Syria/Aram] captured the city of Elathus on *Erythra thalassē*, and he settled Syrians [Heb: Arameans or Edomites; LXX: Idumeans] in Elath."[19]
	Eusebius, *Onomasticon* 6/6:17	"The site of Elath[20] lies near the southern end of Palestine and the *erythra thalassa* and it is accessible by ship both from Egypt and India."
	Epiphanius, *Panarion haereses* 66.1.9–10	One port on *erythra thalassa* that connected India by sea with Egypt was known as Aela, "also known in the sacred scriptures as 'Elath,' where Solomon's ships docked every three years" (1 Kgs 10:22).

18. Cf. 2 Kgs 14:22 reads "Uzziah (son of Amaziah) built Elath and restored it to Judah"; 2 Chr 26:2 reads "Uzziah (son of Amaziah) built Eloth and restored it to Judah" (and cf. 2 Chr 26:6–8 in the context of Philistine, Arab, and Ammonite opponents). Here the "Red Sea" is mentioned neither by the MT, the LXX, nor the Vulgate, so the reference to *erythra thalassa* is found exclusively in Josephus; again Fritz makes no reference to this Josephus citation.

19. Cf. 2 Kgs 16:5–9 (see also 15:37; Isa 7:1, 5–6). Note that Fritz also references this military incident against Jerusalem (see *Lost Sea of Exodus* [2016], 44), but again he makes no mention of the related Josephus text that, unlike either the MT or LXX/Vulgate, also plainly declares that Elath was located "on erythra thalassa."

20. His text reads "Elam," but his reference to the placement of the Tenth Roman Legion at that location provides unmistakable indication that the similar-sounding Elath is intended; furthermore, Eusebius adds that the place is now called "Aila." Note that Jerome also understood Eusebius to mean Elath, using Ailath here in his Latin translation of Eusebius.

Location	Citation	Translation / Summary
	Theodoret, *Questiones in libros Regnorum et Paralipomenon* 80.777.37–40; *Interpretatio in Divini Jeremiae Prophetiam* 91.736.35–36	In both texts Theodoret unambiguously states that "Aila is located at the mouth/entrance of *erythra thalassa*."
	Philostorgios, *Ecclesiastical History* 3.6	"*Mare rubrum* extends a great distance and divides into two gulfs; one gulf touches Egypt at Klysma [Gulf of Suez], where it terminates and from which it receives its name; the other gulf touches Palestine at the city known as Elath since ancient times [Gulf of Aqaba/Elat]."
	Pliny the Elder, *Natural History* 5.12.65	"The two gulfs of *Rubrum mare*, where it converges on Egypt are called Heroopoliticus [Gulf of Suez] and Aelaniticus [Gulf of Aqaba/Elat] … between the towns of Aelana and Gaza, located on the Mediterranean Sea, there is a space of 150 miles (241.5 km) [modern airline distance is 143 miles (230 km)]."
	Procopius of Caesarea, *History of the Wars* 1.19–26	"The boundaries of Palestine extend eastward to the sea called *erythra thalassa*; this *thalassa* begins in India and comes to an end at this point in the Roman domain. Here one finds a city called Aila on its shore, where the sea comes to an end and from which Roman vessels depart."

Thus, one must conclude with certainty that classical authors hailing from widely differing homelands and at varying periods of time repeatedly use the expressions *erythra thalassa* or *mare rubrum* to identify with specificity a variety of modern water bodies, including the Gulf of Aqaba/Elat. I further submit this clear and countervailing evidence stands in polar opposition to the absolute assertion made by Fritz that the Gulf of Aqaba/Elat was materially unknown throughout the classical period and thus was never so referenced in this literature. Unfortunately for Fritz, his hypothesis is not supported by the facts. It appears to me that Fritz is out of touch with classical scholarship in this regard.

3.2 CLASSICAL EXPLORATION SOURCES

Beyond direct textual citations, early Greek exploration of *erythra thalassa* also contains relevant information. Classical literature records as many as a dozen rather detailed nautical reconnaissance missions on the Red Sea, mostly within the eastern sector and, in some cases, into the Gulf of Aqaba/Elat. These missions were conducted by Alexander the Great and the early Ptolemies for purposes of war preparations, procurement of valuable natural resources, commerce, and geographical science.[21] Several of the missions provide unmistakable geographic information directly impacting upon Fritz's hypothesis two, but I shall restrict myself to only one such undertaking, which should serve as a sufficient, unambiguous indication of what was an actual pattern of classical exploration.[22]

These nautical reconnaissance missions commence with Alexander the Great. Almost as soon as Alexander returned to Babylon in early 323 BC from his eastern campaign to the edges of India, the Macedonian monarch began to make war preparations for his intended invasion of the Arabian Peninsula. Toward that end, and as a means of determining military strategy against what at that time would largely have been *terra incognita*, Alexander set out to

---

21. For a succinct summary, see Steven E. Sidebotham, "Red Sea Trade," *ABD* 5:642–44.

22. Beyond the mission of Anaxicrates referenced here, serious exploration related to the eastern portions of the classical Red Sea and/or the Gulf of Aqaba/Elat was also undertaken by Archias (see Arrian, *Anabasis* 7.20.6–7); Nearchus (see Eratosthenes, frags. 68, 77); Philon (Eratosthenes, frag. 40); Ariston (Diodorus 3.42.1); Androsthenes (Eratosthenes, frag. 94); Timosthenes (Eratosthenes, frags. 97, 134); and Simmias. See also Rostovtzeff, *Social and Economic History of the Hellenistic World*; Bernhard Moritz, *Die Sinaikult in heidnischer Zeit*, Abhandlungen der königlichen Gesellschaft der Wissenschaften zu Göttingen, neue folge 16/2 [Berlin: Weidmann, 1916]; Tarn, "Ptolemy II and Arabia"; Stanley J. Burstein, *Agatharchides of Cnidus: On the Erythraean Sea* (London: Hakluyt Society, 1989); and Thomas, "Port Communities and the Erythraean Sea Trade," 169–99.

circumnavigate the peninsula simultaneously from either side.[23] On
the one hand, he ordered Hieron, a naval commander, to sail his fleet
clockwise from Basra (near Babylon) to the vicinity of Heroonpolis
(the classical name for T. el-Maskhuta) in Egypt.[24] On the other,
Alexander determined to explore the peninsula from the opposite
direction, beginning at Heroonpolis, with a fleet presumably under
the command of Anaxicrates, another of Alexander's veteran admirals.
His strategy suggests Alexander intended that his two fleets should
meet somewhere in the middle of their voyages, but this never happened (see map 5). According to Alexander's primary historians,[25]
Hieron traveled only as far as Ra's Musandam (modern Oman, at the
Strait of Hormuz), from where he was obliged to return to Babylon,
and Anaxicrates' mission made it only as far as Bab el-Mandab (the
strait between modern Yemen and Djibouti), where lack of supplies
and good water forced him to reverse course and return to Egypt.
Despite never achieving Alexander's grand objectives, Anaxicrates'
exploration is nevertheless thought to have been very successful, if
only because it provides the earliest source of exact geographical
information having to do with the total length of *erythra thalassa*
(14,000 stades = 1,312 statute miles [2,111.46 km]), measured sig-
nificantly, as we will see just below, from the head of the Gulf of
Aqaba/Elat, not from the Gulf of Suez (the actual marine distance
between modern Aqaba and Bab el-Mandab is 1,325 statute miles
[2,132.4 km]).[26]

---

23. Cf. Pliny, *Natural History* 12.42.86; see also Strabo, *Geography* 15.1.4–19.

24. Donald B. Redford, "Pithom," *LÄ* 4:1054–55; David F. Graf, "The Origin of the
Nabataeans," *Aram* 2 (1990): 66.

25. Diodorus of Sicily, *Bibliotheca Historica*, 3.42.1; Arrian, *Indica*, 43.7 (cf. *Anabasis*,
7.20.8); Quintus Curtius, *Historiae Alexandri Magni*; see also Plutarch, *Life of Alexander*, 75.40;
Theophrastus, *Historia Plantarum* 9.4.2–4.

26. Thus, e.g., Burstein, *Agatharchides of Cnidus*, 2–3; Himanshu Prabha Ray, *The
Archaeology of Seafaring in Ancient South Asia*, Cambridge World Archaeology (Cambridge:
Cambridge University Press, 2003), 169–70. Refer also to Suzanne Amigues, "Anaxikrates'
Expedition to Western Arabia," in *A Gateway from the Eastern Mediterranean to India: The Red
Sea in Antiquity*, ed. Marie-Françoise Boussac and Jean-François Salles (New Delhi: Manohar,
2005), 189–95; Tarn, "Ptolemy II and Arabia," 13, regards the fourteen thousand stades figure

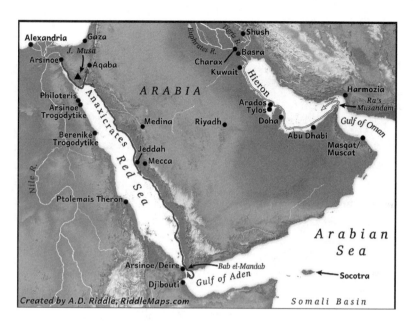

MAP 5: **Alexandrian reconnaissance**

This brings me to the classical figure Eratosthenes. After as many as twenty years studying and writing in Athens, Eratosthenes moved to Alexandria around 240 BC, where Ptolemy III Euergetes had invited him to accept what was probably the most coveted intellectual post in all the Greek world: chief librarian of the Alexandrian library. There Eratosthenes inherited a sizable body of accumulated geographical knowledge collected by the four or five generations of his predecessors. Though Eratosthenes is also known for distinguished scholarship in the creation of a calendar (later appropriated by Julius Caesar) and in astronomy, the crowning achievement of Eratosthenes

---

to be "a measurement extraordinarily creditable to the expedition." In two other texts, Strabo (*Geography* 1.2.28; 2.3.5) uses the figure of fifteen thousand stades for the total length of the gulf, which figure Fritz ("Lost Sea of Exodus" [2006], 100) wrongly attributes to Anaxicrates (and see the citation of Eratosthenes used in my next section), in a further effort to show that the Gulf of Aqaba/Elat lay beyond classical knowledge and exploration.

was his seminal work, *Geographika,* which is said to be the very beginning of the discipline of geography itself.[27]

The ancient geographer's work survives today in numerous fragments of varying length, collected for the most part in three major
sources. Fragment 95 of the *Geographika* presents Eratosthenes'
account of Arabia and the Arabian Gulf, which is the earliest extant
and is an account that is generally thought to have an authentic, eye-
witness historical quality.[28] After a fairly detailed presentation of both
sides of the Arabian Gulf, with its "two recesses," this "father of geography" ends his description with the coastline and the inhabitants of
Arabia, and he concludes:

> Aelana [Aila/Aqaba] is a city on the far recess of the Arabian
> Gulf [i.e., farther away from Alexandria], the recess near Gaza,
> called Aelanites ... that part of the Arabian Gulf along the side
> of Arabia begins with the Aelanites Gulf [*apo tou Ailanitou
> mychou*] and, *as recorded by Alexander's associates and especially
> by Anaxicrates,* extends some 14,000 stades. (emphasis added)[29]

This fragment therefore makes explicit the source of Eratosthenes'
calculation of the total length of the gulf, and it definitively identifies the northern terminus of his calculation. At the same time, this
entire fragment makes clear that Eratosthenes understood the northern extremity of the Arabian Gulf to consist of "two recesses" [*dittos
d'estin*], each identified by name and discrete geographical definition:

---

27. Ronald F. Abler, John S. Adams, and Peter Gould, *Spatial Organization: The Geographer's
View of the World* (Englewood Cliffs, NJ: Prentice-Hall, 1971), 63. The most comprehensive
research relating to the work and writings of Eratosthenes is found in Duane W. Roller,
*Eratosthenes' Geography: Fragments Collected and Translated with Commentary and Additional
Material* (Princeton: Princeton University Press, 2010).

28. Cf. Strabo, *Geography* 16.4.2–4.

29. Eratosthenes, *Geographika,* frag. 95 (Roller, *Eratosthenes' Geography,* 195–97; see also
263–67); cf. the pertinent discussion of E. H. Bunbury, *A History of Ancient Geography: Among
the Greeks and Romans from the Earliest Ages Till the Fall of the Roman Empire* 2 vols. (New
York: Dover, 1959), 1:646-47.

one—called Aelanites, after the city situated on it—extended into the region near Arabia and Gaza, the other reached into the region of Egypt in the vicinity of Heroonpolis (cf. Strabo, *Geography* 2.14.18; Pliny, *Natural History* 6.108; Diodorus 3.42.1). Fritz's notion of a "single gulf near Egypt" is unmistakably refuted by an evidentiary trail that courses through numerous classical sources.

3.3 TRAJAN'S CONSTRUCTION OF THE *VIA NOVA TRAIANA*

With his presumably peaceful annexation of Nabatea/Arabia, Petraea/ Arabia, and Nabatea/Arabia of the Nabateans[30] in the year AD 106, together with the concurrent formation of *Provincia Arabia*, the powerful Roman emperor Trajan gained direct access to the natural resources of a new province (especially aromatics, precious metals, and wood) and—perhaps even more promising—he secured a coveted, more convenient passageway for Roman trade with the mysterious Arabian Peninsula and uninterrupted nautical access to the rich and exotic land of India. As a consequence, Trajan almost immediately undertook to create a first-class, north-south, fully-paved arterial highway (*Via Nova Traiana*, hereafter *VNT*), stretching southward from Damascus in Syria—via the cities of Bostra, Philadelphia/ Amman, Kir-hareseth/Karak, and Petra—as far as Aila/Aqaba on the Gulf of Aqaba/Elat. An achievement celebrated in antiquity and modernity alike,[31] this transportation artery stretched a distance of some 267 miles (427 km = 490 Roman miles).

---

30. Cf., e.g., Diodorus 19.94.1; 51.7.1 (c. 85–21 BC); Strabo, *Geography* 17.1.23 (c. 63 BC–AD 24); Pliny, *Natural History* 5.12.65; 5.15.72 (c. AD 23–79); Plutarch, *Ant.* 36.3 (c. AD 46–120). That is to say, these political/geographical designations were all in existence prior to the time of Trajan.

31. Cf. Galen, *Methodus medendi* 9.8 (633K); Cassius Dio, *Roman History* 68.13.1–5; Avi-Yonah calls this "the greatest piece of Roman road-working in the Orient" (*Holy Land*, 183). This is the only continental highway across Transjordan depicted in the famous Roman cartograph, the Peutinger Map.

MAP 6: **The route of the *Via Nova Traiana* from Damascus to Aqaba/Aila**

The strategic imperative of all segments of what was to become a new consular highway is reflected in the fact that the chief bulwark of Roman imperialism—the legionary army—was almost immediately moved into position at various staging points along the *VNT* and remained present there in one form or another for more than five hundred years. Thus, for example, part or all of the Legion III Cyrenaica was transferred by Trajan from Egypt to Bostra in the early second century, probably as early as AD 107. Not long thereafter, either during the Trajanic imperium or quite early in the Hadrianic era, Legion VI Ferrata was repositioned from either Samosata or Raphanaea in Syria, possibly to the installation/fortress of Udruh, just east of Petra. Moreover, before the end of the second century, auxiliary detachments of Legion III Gallica had been deployed along the highway at the ancient site of Phaina/al-Mismiya, about thirty-one miles (50 km) south-southeast of Damascus. In due course, apparently before the end of the third century, the newly raised IV Martia had deployed to Betthorus/el-Lejjun, just east of Karak, and Legion X Fretensis had been relocated from Jerusalem to Aila/Aqaba.[32]

---

32. See Rami G. Khouri and Donald Whitcomb, *Aqaba: "Port of Palestine on the China Sea"* (Amman: Al Kutba, 1988), 10. Contemporary scholarship generally holds that the site of Aila/Aqaba was founded by the Nabateans, most likely in the late first century BC, and was used for Nabatean maritime trade. See most recently, Ariel S. Lewin, "Rome's Relations with the Arab/Indigenous People in the First–Third Centuries," in *Inside and Out: Interactions between Rome and the Peoples on the Arabian and Egyptian Frontiers in Late Antiquity*, ed. Jitse H. K. Dijkstra and Greg Fisher, Late Antique History and Religion 8 (Leuven: Peeters, 2014), 113–43. Strabo (*Geography* 16.2.30) describes Aila as a *polis* (the terminus of a sixty-day journey from South Africa), and Pliny (*Natural History* 5.12.65) refers to the site as an *oppidum* (a large fortified settlement). The rich archaeological profile of Aila/Aqaba is extensively recorded in the many significant publications of S. Thomas Parker. Thus, e.g., refer to his bibliography in Parker, "Projecting Power on the Periphery: Rome's Arabian Frontier East of the Dead Sea," in *Crossing Jordan: North American Contributions to the Archaeology of Jordan*, ed. Thomas E. Levy et al. (London: Equinox, 2007), 349–57; Parker, "The Roman Port of Aila: Economic Connections with the Red Sea Littoral," in *Connected Hinterlands: Proceedings of Red Sea Project IV Held at the University of Southampton, September 2008*, ed. Lucy Blue et al., Society for Arabian Studies Monographs 8, BARIS 2052 (Oxford: Archaeopress, 2009), 79–84. One should also consult the work of the Oriental Institute of the University of Chicago. See in this regard Donald Whitcomb, "Islamic Archaeology," in *The Oriental Institute 2002–2003 Annual Report* (Chicago: University of Chicago, 2003), https://oi.uchicago.edu/sites/oi.uchicago.edu/files/uploads/shared/docs/ar/01-10/02-03/02-03_Islamic_Arch.pdf.

FIGURE 7: **The Monastery (El Deir) at Petra**

El Deir ("the Monastery"), one of the most magnificent rock carvings in the Nabatean city of Petra, is perched atop a high mountain to the northwest of the site. Thought to have originally been carved as the tomb of a Nabatean king, the building's façade measures 158' (48 m) in width, 154' (47 m) in height, and the building is cut about 80' (26 m) deep into the mountaintop. (Photo by Barry J. Beitzel)

Telltale signs of the actual course of the *VNT* between Petra and Aila have been located, including walled forts and interior structures, reservoirs, aqueducts, a Roman bridge, and the Trajanic triumphal arch at Petra. Actual traces of the paved roadway itself have been reported at different locations by modern researchers—including short stretches with an exposed upper dressing composed of well-ground basalt, laminated over an upper layer of beaten clay, with an outer tier of anchor stones.[33]

---

33. See in this regard the work of Howard Crosby Butler, "Trajan's Road from Boṣra to the Red Sea: The Section between Boṣra and 'Ammân," in *Publications of the Princeton University Archaeological Expeditions to Syria in 1904–05 and 1909; Vol. 4, Division 3: Greek and Latin Inscriptions in Syria, Section A; Southern Syria; Part 2: Southern Haurân: Appendix*, ed. Enno Littmann, David Magie Jr., and Duane Reed Stuart, 7 vols. (Leiden: Brill, 1910), vii–xvi; Butler, "Desert Syria, the Land of a Lost Civilization," *Geographical Review* 9.2 (1920): 77–108. Cf. also

But it is the numerous milestones that most clearly mark both the actual alignment of the highway and most plainly signal the artery's strategic value to the Roman imperium. To date, nearly 275 milestones have been discovered in close proximity to the *VNT* between the sites of Bostra and Aila/Aqaba. None antedate Trajan, despite many earlier stones in Palestine and some in Lebanon. Some forty-two of these milestones have been found in the southernmost segment, between Petra and Aila/Aqaba.

At least twenty-five complete Trajanic milestones or fragmentary specimens along this transportation artery—all dating between AD 111–114 and discovered at find spots ranging from the vicinity of Bostra to Aila/Aqaba—contain a formulaic inscription that is of seminal relevance to my study here: *viam novam a finibus Syriae usque ad mare rubrum aperuit et stravit* ("a new highway, from the border of Syria as far as *mare rubrum*, was opened and paved"; see table 4 and map 6). The majority of these specimens remain in the field, presumably at or near the spot of their original placement.

The following table presents data from datable milestones[34] from Trajan's reign that contain a standard inscribed formula *viam novam*

David F. Graf, "The *Via Nova Traiana* in Arabia Petraea," in *The Roman and Byzantine East: Some Recent Archaeological Research*, ed. John H. Humphrey, JRASup 14 (Ann Arbor: Journal of Roman Archaeology, 1995); Parker, *Rome and the Arabian Frontier: From the Nabataeans to the Saracens* (Brookfield, VT: Ashgate , 1997); Parker, "The *Via Militaris* in Arabia," *DOP* 51 (1997): 271–81; Parker, "Roman Roads East of the Jordan," in *The Madaba Map Centenary 1897–1997: Travelling Through the Byzantine Umayyad Period*, ed. Michele Piccirillo and Eugenio Alliata (Jerusalem: Studium Biblicum Franciscanum, 1999), 230–34; Joan E. Taylor and Shimon Gibson, "Qumran Connected: The Qumran Pass and Paths of the North-Western Dead Sea," in *Qumran und die Archäologie: Texte und Kontexte*, ed. Jörg Frey, Carsten Claussen, and Nadine Kessler, WUNT 278 (Tübingen: Mohr Siebeck, 2011), 163–208.

34. Some of the twenty-five milestones (*milliaria*) listed here contain essentially the entire formula (e.g., AD 111, 14149[21]; 14149[30]; AD 112 [Graf, "*Via Nova*," 38]; AD 114, BD 2:316), while others include sufficient portions in context so as reasonably to permit their inclusion here (e.g., AD 111, 14149[19]; 14149[39]; 14149[42]; 14149[50]; AD 112 [Graf, "*Via Nova*," 30]; AD 114, BD 2:312); see also Thomas Bauzou, "Les voies de communications dans le Hauran à l'époque romaine," in *Hauran I: recherches archéologiques sur la Syrie du Sud à l'époque hellénistique et romaine*, ed. J.-M. Dentzer (Paris: P. Geuthner, 1985), 155 (004); Bauzou, "La *via nova* en Arabie. Le secteur nord, de Bostra à Philadelphie," in *Fouilles de Khirbet es-Samra en Jordanie I*, ed. J.-B. Humbert and A. Desreumaux, Bibliothèque de l'antiquité tardive (Turnhout: Brepols, 1998), 111 (004); David Magie Jr., "Milestones Found on Trajan's Road between Boṣra and 'Ammân," in Littman,

a finibus Syriae usque ad mare rubrum aperuit et stravit.[35] The milestones are sequenced here chronologically and then arranged geographically from north to south. The numbers refer to the sequence of presentation in this table.

Magie, and Stuart, *Publications of the Princeton University Archaeological Expeditions to Syria,* (I). Despite the fact that Trajan most likely transferred part or all of Legion III Cyrenaica from Egypt to Bostra as early as AD 107, it appears from date formulas on the milestones themselves that the earliest actual construction of the *Via Nova* in *Provincia Arabia* was undertaken near the center of the new province. Cf. Maurice Sartre, "Nouvelles Inscriptions Grecques et Latines de Bostra," *AAAS* 22 (1972): 172–73; Michael Alexander Speidel, "The Roman Army in Arabia," *ANRW* 2.8:689–97. Thus, e.g., work on the highway between Petra and Philadelphia/Amman is dated by milestones to the year AD 111, the southern section between Petra and Aqaba dates to AD 112, whereas the northernmost section between Amman and Bostra dates to AD 114. See Thomas Bauzou, "A Finibus Syriae: Recherches sur les routes des frontièrs orientales de l'Empire Romain," 3 vols. (PhD diss. Université de Paris I, Institut d'Art et d'Archéologie, 1989), 1:151 n. 39; S. Thomas Parker, "The Roman 'Aqaba Project: The 1994 Campaign," *ADAJ* 40 (1996): 234. It may be that work began around Petra because Rome had just annexed the province after the death of the Nabatean king of Petra—Rabbel II Soter—in AD 106. In any event, one observes that where *millia passuum* (MP) distances are legible on Trajanic milestones, both earlier (e.g., ##5, 8) and later (e.g., #22), the mileage is often calculated from Petra (see also Bauzou, "La *via nova*," 239). See also Jacqueline Calzini Gysens, "Interim Report on the Rabbathmoab and Qaṣr Rabbah Project," *East and West* 58 (2008): 60, with reference to *CIL* 14149[41] (found at same location as my #4, but dating to AD 162 [Marcus Aurelius]), which shows an MP in *millia* from Petra.

35. Remarkably similar wording appears on Trajanic milestones discovered elsewhere in the imperium (e.g., in north central Italy [*via nova Traianam a Volsinis ad fines Clusinorum fecit*; "(PN) built a new Traiana road from Bolsena to the border of Clusium/Chiusi"], dated to the year AD 108. This paved road stretched from Lake Bolsena to modern Chiusi, where it joined the *Via Cassia* (see *BAGRW*, map 42 [B3]); William Thayer, "The Road Is Gone and as Often, Only the Milestone Remains," http://penelope.uchicago.edu/Thayer/E/Gazetteer/Places/Europe/Italy/Umbria/Terni/Orvieto/Orvieto/Roman/milestone.html.

TABLE 4: Evidence from Trajan's dated milestones along the *Via Nova Traiana*

No.	Data[36]	Find Spot and Description	Bibliography
#1	Date: AD 111(?) ID: 14155 MP: [ ]	Discovered among ruins near the southern gate of Khirbet es-Suq, c. 5.5 miles (9 km) S of Amman/Philadelphia, between Umm Quṣeir and al-Yaduda, on the *Via Nova*;[37] this is a very fragmentary text, lacking date and MP; the first few lines contain a fairly standard Trajanic formula, including most of the emperor's name (TRAIAN[us]); however, the identity of Trajan is disputed: Germer-Durand and Borstad ascribe this stone to Trajan Decius and thus date it to the mid-third century.[38] On the other hand, Brünnow and Domaszewski, Thomsen, and especially Graf attribute the stone to Nerva Trajan.[39] While uncertainty is unavoidable, the stone's find spot at this point along the *Via Nova*, on the view of Brünnow and Domaszewski and that of Thomsen, makes an AD 111 date quite plausible.	*CIL* 3.2312=BD 2:179 (25c).[40]

36. This column includes the date of the milestone, its identifying siglum (ID) in the relevant publications, and its MP marking. MP can sometimes be reconstructed from other milestones found in the same location. Note the siglum relates to its identifying information in the first publication listed under "Bibliography."

37. Note *TBA* B/VI/10, just north of al-Yaduda, a milestone find spot is marked on the map.

38. R. P. Germer-Durand, "Exploration épigraphique de Gerasa," *RB* 4.3 (1895): 398; Karen A. Borstad, "History from Geography: The Initial Route of the *Via Nova Traiana* in Jordan," *Levant* 40 (2008): 64.

39. BD 2:23; Peter Thomsen, "Die römischen Meilensteine der Provinzen Syria, Arabia und Palaestina," *ZDPV* 40 (1917): 47; Graf, "*Via Militaris*," 274.

40. Germer-Durand, "Exploration," 398; cf. Thomsen, "Meilensteine," 47 (113, dated by him to the year AD 114?); see Graf, "*Via Militaris*," fig 1, for a map placement of my stones ##1–8.

No.	Data	Find Spot and Description	Bibliography
#2	Date: AD 111 ID: 14149⁵⁰ MP: [ ]	Discovered near the W. Wâleh/Heidan.⁴¹ Therefore, this find spot must be very near the intersection point of W. Wâleh/Heidan and the *Via Nova*, or in the vicinity of classical Valtha (4.35 miles [7 km] S of Libb).⁴² The first seven lines are nearly complete, which include the date; nevertheless, this is a fairly fragmentary stone, lacking the MP.	*CIL* 3.2309=BD 1:29 (3e[32a]).⁴³
#3	Date: AD 111 ID: 14149³⁹ MP: XVI	Discovered near the Arnon Gorge (W. Mojib).⁴⁴ This is a nearly complete specimen with minimal wear, bearing both date and MP.	*CIL* 3.2308=*ILS* 2.1:439 (5845ᵃ)=BD 1:42 (4b[33a]).⁴⁵
#4	Date: AD 111 ID: 14149⁴² MP: [ ]	Discovered near the Arnon Gorge (cf. #3); Bauzou and Borstad note that this stone was found at the same location with *CIL* 14149⁴¹ (Marcus Aurelius, AD 162) and *CIL* 14149⁴³ (Pertinax, AD 194), suggestive of sustained road development at that location.⁴⁶ This is a fairly fragmentary stone, lacking date and MP; standard Trajanic formula.	*CIL* 3.2308=BD 1:38 (4b[9b]).⁴⁷

41. *Atlas of Israel: Cartography, Physical and Human Geography*, 3rd ed. (Tel Aviv: Survey of Israel, 1985), map I/11 [N21]; see also Ahmed Abdulla Gharaibeh, "Heat Source Study and Geothermal Reservoir Assessment for the Zarqa Ma'in—Dab'a Area, Central Jordan," *United Nations University, Reports* 17 (2008): 231–33.

42. *BAGRW* map 71 [B2]; and see *TBA* B/V/18 for milestones near Valtha.

43. Cf. Thomsen, "Meilensteine," 49 (121a); Negev, "Nabateans," 646; Bauzou, "Finibus," 2:464 (166); Borstad, "History," 66; Gysens, "Interim Report," 60.

44. See *TBA* B/V/18 for milestones near Arnon.

45. Cf. Thomsen, "Meilensteine," 51 (127a₁); Bauzou, "Finibus," 2:478 (180); Borstad, "History," 66. For an early black and white photograph of the upper portion of this stone, see C. Preaux, "Une source nouvelle sur l'annexion de l'Arabie par Trajan: Les papyrus de Michigan 465 et 466," *Phoibos* 5 (1950–1951): pl. IX.

46. Bauzou, "Finibus," 2:474; Borstad, "History," 64.

47. Cf. Thomsen, "Meilensteine," 50 (126b₁); Bauzou, "Finibus," 2:472–73 (175); Borstad, "History," 66.

No.	Data	Find Spot and Description	Bibliography
#5	Date: AD 111 ID: 14149[30] MP: LIX	Discovered between Dhāt-Ra's and Thornia/Thoana (at-Tuwāna), 59 Roman miles (54.3 miles; 87.4 km) N of Petra.[48] This is an almost complete specimen, bearing both date and MP.[49]	CIL 3.2307=BD 1:83 (6[3.46a]).[50]
#6	Date: AD 111 ID: 14149[29] MP: [ ]	Discovered 58 Roman miles (53 miles; 86 km) N of Petra (cf. #5); this is an extremely fragmentary stone, lacking date and MP.[51]	CIL 3:2306=BD 1:84 (6[4.4]).[52]
#7	Date: AD 111 ID: 14149[21] MP: [ ]	Discovered between Dhāt-Ra's and Thornia/Thoana (at-Tuwāna), in the W. Qleita, 54 Roman miles (50 miles; 80 km) N of Petra (cf. #6). This is a nearly complete specimen, arguably the best preserved inscription from this year, bearing date and lacking MP.[53]	CIL 3:2306=BD 1:85 (6 [5.12a]).[54]

48. See *BAGRW* map 71 (B3); *TBA* map B/V/18 (31.00/35.30) (2192.0182); *Atlas of Israel* map 1/12 (P26).

49. This appears to be site #384 in Burton MacDonald, Gary O. Rollefson, and Duane W. Roller, "The Wadi el-Hasa Survey 1981: A Preliminary Report," *ADAJ* (1982): 452 (pl 31).

50. Cf. Thomsen, "Meilensteine," 52 (138a); Germer-Durand, "Exploration," 84; Bauzou, "Finibus," 2:488 (192); Borstad, "History," 66.

51. This appears to be site #406 in MacDonald, Rollefson, and Roller, "Wadi el-Hasa."

52. Cf. Thomsen, "Meilensteine," 52 (139); Germer-Durand, "Exploration," 583; Bauzou, "Finibus," 2:489–90 (194); Borstad, "History," 66.

53. This appears to be site #409 in MacDonald, Rollefson, and Roller, "Wadi el-Hasa."

54. Cf. Thomsen, "Meilensteine," 53 (143a); see also Magie, "Milestones," xvii–xxviii (between Petra and Amman); Germer-Durand, "Exploration," 581; Bauzou, "Finibus," 2:492–93 (198); Borstad, "History," 66; Thomas Pekáry, *Untersuchungen zu den römischen Reichsstrassen*, Antiquitas. Abhandlungen zur alten Geschichte 17 (Bonn: Habelt, 1968), 140.

No.	Data	Find Spot and Description	Bibliography
#8	Date: AD 111 ID: 14149[19] MP: LI	Discovered between Dhāt-Raʿs and Thornia/Thoana (at-Tuwāna), 51 Roman miles (47 miles; 75.6 km) N of Petra (cf. #7); the final five lines are nearly complete, including MP, and it is clearly a Trajanic stone, though beyond that the text appears quite fragmentary lacking date.[55]	*CIL* 3:2305=*ILS* 2.1:436 (5834)=BD 1:86 (6 [6.2a]).[56]
#9	Date: AD 112 ID: 30 MP: [ ]	Discovered c. 7 Roman miles (6 miles; 9.8 km) S of Quweira, just S of the entrance to W. Ramm and only a few yards/meters E of the old road to Aqaba; only the first few lines are legible, lacking date and MP, but it is clearly Trajanic.	Graf, "*Via Nova*," 59 (fig 14); Graf, "*Via Militaris*," VI:25 (fig 14).[57]
#10	Date: AD 112(?) ID: 34 MP: [ ]	Discovered c. 10 Roman miles (9 miles; 14.5 km) S of Quweira, near Khalde, near the entrance to W. Yutm, along the E side; only part of the first few lines legible, lacking date and MP, but it is clearly Trajanic.	Graf, "*Via Nova*," 258–59; Graf, "*Via Militaris*," VI.25-27.[58]

55. This may be site #413 in MacDonald, Rollefson, and Roller, "Wadi el-Hasa."

56. Cf. Thomsen, "Meilensteine," 53 (146a); Germer-Durand, "Exploration," 580; Bauzou "Finibus," 2:498–99 (205); Borstad, "History," 65.

57. Cf. Albrecht Alt, "Studien aus dem Deutschen evang. Institut für Altertumswissenschaft in Jerusalem," *ZDPV* 59 (1936): 99–100. Alt's inscription probably dates to the late third century, but Graf's Trajanic inscription was found on the opposite side of the same stone.

58. A. Jaussen, "Voyage du Sinai," *RB* 12 (1903): 101, 106 (found between the plain of el-Mezraʿah and el-Medifein); Thomsen, "Meilensteine," 57 (175a), dates the text to AD 111; Alois Musil, *Arabia Petraea*, 3 vols., Kaiserliche Akademie der Wissenschaften (Vienna: Hölder, 1907–1908), 2:263, found in the W. Yutm (and see fig. 142); Alt, "Studien," 100–101; Bauzou dates the text to AD 111. See Bauzou, "Finibus," 2:211–12 (221).

No.	Data	Find Spot and Description	Bibliography
#11	Date: AD 112 ID: 38 MP: [ ]	Discovered near Kh. al-Kithara, 12 Roman miles (11 miles; 17.8 km) NE of Aqaba. This stone was found in the garden of the Jordanian Coast Guard in 1988.[59] This is a nearly complete specimen, including date and lacking MP, with minimal wear, and the stone remains in a good state of preservation (displayed today in the Aqaba Archaeological Museum).[60]	Graf, "Via Nova," 261–62 (and fig 17); Graf, "Via Militaris," VI: 28-29 (and fig 17).
#12	Date: AD 112(?) ID: 39 MP: [ ]	Discovered at the same find spot as #11; only the first few lines are legible, but it is clearly Trajanic; the stone lacks date and MP.	Graf, "Via Nova," 261; Graf, "Via Militaris," VI:28.
#13	Date: AD 114 ID: BD 2:312 (7.9a) MP: [CXCVIII]	Discovered 198 Roman miles (182.3 miles; 293.4 km) N of Petra = 9 Roman miles (8.3 miles; 13.3 km) SW of Bostra; this is a very fragmentary stone, lacking date and MP, but it is clearly Trajanic.	Thomsen, "Meilensteine," 37 (71a).[61]

59. Cf. Henry Innes MacAdam, *Studies in the History of the Roman Province of Arabia: The Northern Sector,* BARIS 295 (Oxford: BAR, 1986), 172. No record of its original find spot is known, but Graf was informed that it was moved to the Aqaba Marina from Kh. al-Kithara during the 1950s (Graf, "Via Nova," 261). Another milestone was found at the Marina, fragmented and bearing only the first several lines of a Trajanic formula (Graf, "Via Nova," 261 [39]).

60. Additional information on milestone #11 (as well as the Trajanic milestone fragment referenced by Graf, "Via Nova," 261 [39]) was kindly supplied by Donald Whitcomb, Director of the University of Chicago/Jordanian Department of Antiquities joint expedition team in 1988 (personal correspondence, 10/11/11). Whitcomb states: "The two milestones were found in the garden of the Jordanian Coast Guard camp (abandoned in 1988). During that year our expedition, the Medieval Aqaba Project, cleaned the stones (which had thick coats of white paint) and made copies and photos. The stones had been set up in the former Arab Legion camp (later the Transjordanian Frontier Force), probably in the 1940s. There is no record of the original findspot of the stones; they [may] be from Aqaba itself or brought from any mile along the road ... I am fairly certain that the better of the stones is on display in the Aqaba museum" [which in fact is the case].

61. R. Germer-Durand, "Rapport sur l'exploration archéologique en 1903 de la voie Romaine entre Ammân et Bostra (Arabie)," *Bulletin archéologique du Comité des travaux historiques et scientifiques* 11 (1904): 6/2 (CLXVI). See also Butler, "Trajan's Road," vi, ix; Bauzou, "Finibus," 2:15-16 (04); Bauzou, "La via nova," 110 (001); Bauzou, "Voies," 154 (001); Borstad, "History," 66.

No.	Data	Find Spot and Description	Bibliography
#14	Date: AD 114 ID: 002 MP: [ ]	Discovered 197 Roman miles (181.4 miles; 291.9 km) N of Petra = 10 Roman miles (9.2 miles; 14.8 km) SW of Bostra; this is an extremely fragmentary stone, lacking MP and most of the date, but it is clearly a Trajanic stone, including part of the emperor's name.	Bauzou, "Finibus," 2.338 (357); Bauzou, "La *via nova*," 110 (002); Bauzou, "Voies," 154 (002).
#15	Date: AD 114 ID: 003 MP: [ ]	Discovered 196 Roman miles (180 miles; 290 km) N of Petra = 11 or 12 Roman miles (c. 10 miles; 17 km) SW of Bostra; two very fragmentary pieces, lacking date and MP, but this is clearly Trajanic.	Bauzou, "Finibus," 2:18-19 (08); Bauzou, "La *via nova*," 110 (003); Bauzou, "Voies," 154 (003).
#16	Date: AD 114 ID: 004 MP: [ ]	Discovered 195 Roman miles (180 miles; 289 km) N of Petra = 12 Roman (11 miles; 17.8 km) miles SW of Bostra; aside from five lines in the middle of this stone, including clear Trajanic formulary and date, this is a very fragmentary stone also lacking MP.	Bauzou, "Finibus," 2:23 (13); Bauzou, "La *via nova*," 111 (004); Bauzou, "Voies," 155 (004).
#17	Date: AD 114 ID: I MP: [ ]	Discovered 14 Roman miles (12.9 miles; 20.7 km) SW of Bostra; this is a fairly fragmentary stone, lacking part of the date and containing a garbled MP, but it contains Trajan's name and clearly contains Trajanic formulary.	Magie, "Milestones," xvii (XIV).[62]

---

62. Cf. Thomsen, "Meilensteine," 39 (76a); Germer-Durand, "Rapport," 11/11 (CLXXI). This text contains a garbled date formula (see Magie's almost impossible reading and Germer-Durand's unlikely conclusion) that is most plausibly correctly read by Thomsen. See also Bauzou, "Finibus," 2:3132 (20); Borstad, "History," 66.

No.	Data	Find Spot and Description	Bibliography
#18	Date: AD 114 ID: BD 2:314 (7.14a) MP: [CXCIII]	Discovered 193 Roman miles (178 miles; 286 km) N of Petra = 14 Roman miles (12.9 miles; 20.7 km) SW of Bostra; this is the same location as the preceding stone, but the inscriptions differ; this is a fairly fragmentary stone, lacking date and MP.	Butler, "Trajan's Road," vi; Bauzou, "Finibus," 1:45 (14b).
#19	Date: AD 114(?) ID: IV.A MP: XV	Discovered 15 Roman miles (13.8 miles; 22.2 km) SW of Bostra; this is an extremely fragmentary stone, lacking date but bearing MP. Given the find spot of this extremely fragmented stone, together with its MP, a date of AD 114 is quite likely.	Magie, "Milestones," xix; Thomsen, "Meilensteine," 40 (77a$_3$); Bauzou, "Finibus," 1:46-47.[63]
#20	Date: AD 114 ID: IX.B MP: [ ]	Discovered 17 Roman miles (15.7 miles; 25.2 km) SW of Bostra; with the first three lines intact, this is an extremely fragmentary stone, lacking date and MP, but it is clearly Trajanic.	Magie, "Milestones," xxiii.[64]
#21	Date: AD 114 ID: XIII MP: [ ]	Discovered 18 Roman miles (16.6 miles; 26.7 km) SW of Bostra; this is a fairly fragmentary stone, bearing date and lacking MP, but it is clearly Trajanic.	Magie, "Milestones," xxiv; Thomsen, "Meilensteine," 41 (81a).[65]

63. Note that Magie attributes the milestone to Pertinax, but Thomsen attributes to Trajan and dates c. AD 114.

64. Cf. Thomsen, "Meilensteine," 40 (79b); Bauzou, "Finibus," 2:52 (38); Borstad, "History," 66.

65. See also Butler, "Trajan's Road," xi; Bauzou, "Finibus," 2:56–57 (44); Borstad, "History," 66.

No.	Data	Find Spot and Description	Bibliography
#22	Date: AD 114 ID: BD 2:316 (7.25a) MP: CLXXXII	Discovered 182 Roman miles (167.6 miles; 269.7 km) N of Petra = 25 Roman miles (23 miles; 37 km) SW of Bostra; the upper eight lines are fairly complete, including date; the broken stone also bears an MP; standard Trajanic formulary.	Germer-Durand, "Rapport," 16/22.[66]
#23	Date: AD 114 ID: 009 MP: [ ]	Discovered 181 Roman miles (166.7 miles; 268.2 km) N of Petra = 26 Roman miles (24 miles; 38.5 km) SW of Bostra; this is an extremely fragmentary specimen, with a portion of only a few lines surviving; however, the stone does contain a partial date of Trajan.	Bauzou, "Finibus," 2:93–94 (84); Bauzou, "La via nova," 119 (009); Bauzou, "Voies," 157 (009).
#24	Date: AD 114 ID: BD 2:317 (7.28) MP: [CLXXIX]	Discovered 179 Roman miles (164.8 miles; 265.3 km) N of Petra = 28 Roman miles (25.8 miles; 41.5 km) SW of Bostra; aside from what is found along the right edge, this is a very fragmentary stone, lacking date and MP, but it is clearly a Trajanic stone.	Thomsen, "Meilensteine," 43 (90); Germer-Durand, "Rapport," 20/28 (CLXXXV).[67]
#25	Date: AD 114 ID: 14150[11] MP: [ ]	Discovered 38 Roman miles (35 miles; 56.3 km) SW of Bostra; this is an extremely fragmentary stone, lacking MP and part of the date, but it is clearly a Trajanic stone.	CIL 3.2311=BD 2:226 [30.48].[68]

66. Cf. Thomsen, "Meilensteine," 42 (87a); Butler, "Trajan's Road," xii; Bauzou, "Finibus," 2:84–86 (76); Borstad, "History," 66.

67. See also Butler, "Trajan's Road," vi, xii; Bauzou, "Finibus," 2:103–4 (92); Bauzou, "La via nova," 120 (010); Bauzou, "Voies," 157–58 (010); Borstad, "History," 66.

68. cf. Thomsen, "Meilensteine," 44 (99); Bauzou, "Finibus," 2:114–15); dated by Herman Dessau, ILS 3.2:436 to AD 111; Borstad, "History," 66 (14 Roman miles northeast of Philadelphia).

This formula makes explicit the fact that the *VNT* led to and directly joined the *mare rubrum* (= Gulf of Aqaba/Elat) at the city of Aila/Aqaba.[69] No countervailing evidence exists to suggest that the southernmost stretches of the *VNT* would have veered west at the last minute to the Gulf of Suez or somehow shifted southeast, so as to bypass Aila. One must also observe that Roman Aila sat adjacent to the modern shoreline of the Gulf of Aqaba. Extensive archaeological work conducted at the site over the past twenty-five years has provided clear and substantial architectural and artifactual indication of that city's rich cosmopolitan, commercial heritage as a vital transportation hub during the Roman and early Byzantine periods (see pages 76–77, note 32).

Moreover, the conviction that Trajan's road met the Red Sea at Aila/Aqaba, and not at some other place, is strongly supported by the fact that several of these milestones were found along the Wadi Yutm in the direction of Aqaba, *south* of where the modern road to Ramm, Egra, and Medina diverges southeast. If additional confidence in these data is desired, the security of this conviction becomes even more decisive by virtue of the fact that five of the milestones are thought to have been originally erected in the vicinity of Khirbet al-Kithara, inside the confines of the canyon-like Wadi Yutm and at a site along the road just twelve miles (20 km) northeast of Aqaba, and two of these five were found inside the city of Aqaba itself. Henry MacAdam flatly declares, "'To the Red Sea' can mean only one thing—the road terminated in the far south at the gulf of 'Aqabā, more specifically at

69. This affirmation is anchored in a wide swath of scholarship, including the following works: Pekáry, *Untersuchungen*, 141; Siegfried Mittmann, *Beiträge zur Siedlungs- und Territorialgeschichte des nördlichen Ostjordanlandes*, ADPV (Wiesbaden: Harrassowitz, 1966), 162; Negev, "Nabataeans," 2.8:645–46; Thomas Bauzou, "Les voies romaines entre Damas et Amman," in *Géographie historique au Proche-Orient (Syrie, Phénicie, Arabie, grecques, romaines, byzantines): Actes de la Table Ronde de Valbonne, 16–18 septembre 1985*, ed. Pierre-Louis Gatier, Bruno Helly, and Jean-Paul Rey-Coquais, Notes et monographies techniques, Centre de recherches archéologiques 23 (Paris: Éditions du Centre National de la Recherché Scientifique, 1990), 298 n. 10; Israel Roll, "The Roads in Roman-Byzantine Palaestina and Arabia," in Piccirillo and Alliata, *Madaba Map Centenary*, 109.

	Transcription	Normalized text
1	IMPCAESAR	*Imp(erator) Caesar*
2	DIVINERVAEFNERVA	*divi Nervae f(ilius) Nerva(e)*
3	TRAIANVSAVGGERM	*Traianus Aug(ustus) Germ(anicus)*
4	[D]ACICVSPONTMAXIMVS	*[D]acicus Pont(ifex) Maximus*
5	TRIBPOTXVIMPVICOSV	*trib(unicia) pot(estate) XV, imp(erator) VI, co(n)s(ul) V,*
6	[P]PREDAC[TA]INFORMAM	*[p(ater)] p(atriae), redac[ta] in formam*
7	PROVINCIAEARABIAVIAM	*provinciae Arabia viam*
8	NOVAM[A]FINIBVSSYRIAE	*novam [a] finibus Syriae*
9	VSQVEADMARERVBRVM	*usque ad mare rubrum*
10	[A]PERVITETSTRAVITPER	*[a]peruit et stravit per*
11	CCLAVDIVMSEVERVM	*C(aius) Claudium Severum*
12	LEGAV[GPR]PR	*leg(atum) Au[g(usti) pr(o)] pr(aetore)*
13	[MP]	*[mp]*

Translation

[1]The Emperor Caesar, [2]son of the divine Nerva, Nerva [3]Trajan, the Augustus, Germanicus, [4][D]acicus, Pontifex Maximus, [5]invested for the fifteenth time as Tribune, the sixth time as Emperor, and the fifth time as Consul {i.e., AD 111; see *ILS* 3.1:274–75}, [6][Father] of the Fatherland, having reduc[ed] Arabia to the status [7]of a province, a highway—[8]a new one [from] the border of Syria [9]as far as *mare rubrum*— [10]was [op]ened and paved by [11]Caius Claudius Severus, [12]legate/envoy of the Em[peror and the acting] Praetor. [13][MP {unknown}].

FIGURE 8: **Reading of an inscribed Trajanic milestone**

This is milestone #7 in table 4. The reading is based on my on-site examination of the stone on 3 July 2013. Abbreviations are expanded in parentheses, square brackets mark reconstructions of breaks in the text, and curly braces set off clarifying notes.

FIGURE 9: **Image of an inscribed Trajanic milestone**

Milestone #7 was found lying face-up on the ground, adjacent to a short exposed stretch of the *VNT*. The inscription is traced here for diagnostic purposes (original inscriptions were sometimes painted similarly in red); added lettering in the dirt is intended to show what was visible on the left side of the stone. (Photo by Barry J. Beitzel)

FIGURE 10: **View of Aqaba**

The modern Jordanian city of Aqaba (ancient Aila; Elath) rests on the narrow plain between the northernmost edge of the Gulf of Aqaba/Elat (foreground) and the exposed, elevated pre-Cambrian mountains of Jordan, including Jebel Karifa and Jebel Baqir. (Public Domain)

the port of Aela."[70] A broad-based scholarly acceptance of MacAdam's pronouncement is not at all surprising and is completely understandable.[71] Accordingly, one is justified making the claim that the expression *mare rubrum* had been carried to the very edges of Trajan's imperium and had been sanctioned there by royal imprimatur to apply precisely to the place where the city of Aila/Aqaba adjoined the Gulf of Aqaba/Elat.[72] And given the fact that inscribed milestones

---

70. MacAdam, *Studies in the History of the Roman Province of Arabia*, 21.

71. Cf., e.g., Taylor and Gibson, "Qumran Connected," 166; Khouri and Whitcomb, *Aqaba*, 10; Gysens, "Interim Report," 60; Angelo Di Berardino, ed., *Historical Atlas of Ancient Christianity* (St. Davids, PA: ICCS Press, 2013), 84; Lewin, "Rome's Relations," 125.

72. Tønnes Bekker-Nielsen, *The Roads of Ancient Cyprus* (Copenhagen: Museum Tusculanum Press, 2004), 41, argues that the uniformity of milestone formulas for a certain year are generally the same within a given province, showing that it had been drawn up by the

were created to function seemingly as redundant sentinels of royal pedigree, imperial sovereignty, and military accomplishment—rather than merely as a kind of classical GPS, which could have been accomplished with a great deal less time, flourish, and masonry skill—one might argue that by the time of Trajan, the expression *mare rubrum*, directly linked to the port at Aila/Aqaba, had even come to be considered part of colloquial parlance both throughout the imperium and on the part of the traveling public in general (merchants, military detachments, migrant workers, teachers, pilgrims, and like).[73]

Once again the evidentiary record of classical written sources provides unmistakable indication that the Gulf of Aqaba/Elat was commonly apprehended and repeatedly attested as *erythra thalassa* or *mare rubrum*, had been explored scientifically and traversed commercially from one end to the other, and was known with considerable familiarity in the classical world. The evidence plainly shows that the Gulf of Aqaba/Elat was in no sense lost in the classical world. Such a conclusion is entirely consistent with the studied judgment of J. Oliver Thomson, the highly acclaimed professor of the history of ancient geography, who declares that by the time of Julius Caesar—when Egypt became fully incorporated into the Roman imperial amalgam—"the Red Sea had long been minutely known."[74]

---

provincial governor or his chancellery; Pekáry, *Untersuchungen*, 19, suggests that the wording of milestone inscriptions required the approval of the emperor. In a personal email (9/1/14), Thomas Bauzou declares that the *VNT* formula was probably worded in Rome, possibly by the emperor himself.

73. Cf. Pekáry, *Untersuchungen*, 21, 36; Ray Laurence, *The Roads of Roman Italy: Mobility and Cultural Change* (London: Routledge, 1999), 40; Romolo Augusto Staccioli, *The Roads of the Romans* (Los Angeles: Getty Museum, 2003), 56; Borstad, "History," 58; see now Chaim Ben David, "Milestones near Roman Army Installations in Desert Areas in the Provinces of Palaestina and Arabia," in *Roman Roads: New Evidence—New Perspectives*, ed. Anne Kolb (Berlin: De Gruyter, 2019), 132–46.

74. J. Oliver Thomson, *History of Ancient Geography* (New York: Biblo & Tannen, 1965), 273.

Chapter 4

EVIDENCE FROM EARLY CARTOGRAPHICALLY RELATED SOURCES

E vidence from biblical and classical resources having to do with *yam sûf/erythra thalassa/mare rubrum* can be augmented with early cartographically related sources as well. The history of classical cartography is a field that has accrued a vast bibliography.[1] Touching on a few details relevant to my focus here, I summarize from my own earlier work: Owing to considerable technological and scientific advances in mathematics, astronomy, and philosophy during the classical period, a number of theoretical principles essential to a more refined and exact geographic mapmaking were introduced. Thus, for example, Thales, the famed Greek astronomer and mathematician from Miletus (c. 624–548 BC, fl. 590 BC) is credited with

---

1. For a few selected pieces from a massive bibliography, refer especially to the exhaustive treatment found in J. B. Harley and David Woodward, *The History of Cartography: Cartography in Prehistoric, Ancient and Medieval Europe and the Mediterranean*, 6 vols. (Chicago: University of Chicago Press, 1987–2015); see also P. D. A. Harvey, *The History of Topographical Maps* (London: Thames & Hudson, 1980); O. A. W. Dilke, *Greek and Roman Maps* (Ithaca, NY: Cornell University Press, 1985).

being the first individual to predict eclipses and to calculate the length of the year. Anaximander, the distinguished Greek scientist and philosopher from Miletus (c. 610–546 BC, fl. 575 BC), invented the gnomon and introduced the sundial, and he is thought to be the first person to have drawn an outline of land and sea and to have constructed a globe. Eudoxos, the important Greek astronomer and mathematician from Cnidus (c. 390–337 BC, fl. 360 BC), graphed the elliptical movement of celestial bodies, and he created a globe that included the equator, the tropics, and the arctic circles. Aristotle, the noted Greek philosopher, polymath, and tutor of Alexander the Great (384–322 BC, fl. 350 BC), rationalized the arguments for the sphericity of the earth. Eratosthenes, the brilliant Greek astronomer, mathematician, and revered founder of geography, from Cyrene and Alexandria (c. 276–195 BC, fl. 240 BC), geometrically calculated the length of every parallel circle of the earth, from which he was able to compute the measurement of the circumference of the earth with remarkable accuracy (252,000 stades = 24,663 miles [39,691 km], as over against the modern calculation of 24,902.461 miles [40,076.6 km], finally determined only in the mid-twentieth century, and with the aid of satellite technology). Finally, Claudius Ptolemais (Ptolemy), the extraordinarily famed Greek astronomer, mathematician, and geographer from Alexandria (c. AD 100–170, fl. AD 135), created a grid system of parallels and meridians which made it possible for the first time cartographically to project the spherical world onto a flat surface.[2]

In his massive tome *Geographia*, Ptolemy undertook to formulate a highly technical and statistical manual designed to assist professional cartographers in the creation of accurate and usable maps. It was a daunting attempt to catalog and locate known geographical realia by means of latitudinal and longitudinal coordinates, thus creating the novel invention of a formal grid system. The *Geographia* contains

---

2. Barry J. Beitzel, "Exegesis, Dogmatics and Cartography: A Strange Alchemy in Earlier Church Traditions," *Archaeology in the Biblical World* 2.2 (1994): 9 and n. 4.

an estimated eight thousand tabular entries in eight volumes, and Ptolemy sought to provide locational coordinates as they existed at the time, including geographical entries such as provincial boundaries, cities, rivers, islands, mountains, lakes, various people groups, and the like. In stark contrast to Fritz,[3] who rather quickly dismisses the work of Ptolemy and who even regards it as a prime illustration to show that the Gulf of Aqaba/Elat was still "poorly understood" in the classical era (see below), it is fair to state that contemporary cartographic scholarship in general axiomatically regards Ptolemy's landmark achievement as the high water mark of geography and cartography for some fourteen hundred years, until the time of Mercator.[4]

Table 5 below features all of Ptolemy's work relevant to the Gulf of Aqaba/Elat, the Sinai Peninsula, and contiguous terrain north of the twenty-fourth parallel.[5] The section citations and the coordinates contained in table 5 derive from the standard critical editions—that of Carolus Fredericus Augustus Nobbe, abbreviated N in the table, and that of Alfred Stückelberger and Gerd Grasshoff, abbreviated SG in the table, which are the most recent complete and reliable editions of Ptolemy's Greek text.[6] The location of the Ptolemaic citations in those editions is given in brackets in the table. Edward Stevenson's English edition omits important parts of book 8 and is itself derived from an entirely secondary Latin translation produced by Jacobus Angelus in the early Renaissance period (reflected in part even in

3. Fritz, "Lost Sea of Exodus" (2006), 101, 232–34; Fritz, *Lost Sea of Exodus* (2016), 113, 183, 258.

4. See, e.g., O. A. W. Dilke, "The Culmination of Greek Cartography in Ptolemy," with additional material supplied by the editors, in *Cartography in Prehistoric, Ancient, and Medieval Europe and the Mediterranean*, ed. J. B. Harley and David Woodward, vol. 1 of *The History of Cartography*, ed. J. B. Harley and David Woodward (Chicago: University of Chicago Press, 1987), 177; G. J. Toomer, "Ptolemy," *Complete Dictionary of Scientific Biography* (Detroit: Cengage, 2008), https://www.encyclopedia.com/people/science-and-technology/astronomy-biographies/ptolemy.

5. Ptolemy records no other absolutely identified sites north of the twenty-fourth parallel in northwestern Arabia that are contiguous to the modern Red Sea shoreline.

6. Carolus Fridericus Augustus Nobbe, *Claudii Ptolemaei Geographia* (Leipzig: Tauchnitus, 1843–1845 [= N]) and Alfred Stückelberger and Gerd Grasshoff, *Klaudios Ptolemaios: Handbuch des Geographie, Griechisch-Deutsch* (Basel: Schwabe Verlag, 2006 [= SG]).

Stevenson's title).[7] Stevenson's edition is sadly marred by fatal translational flaws. Aubrey Diller—a renowned scholar of Greek literature and classical cartography—offers a scathing critique of Stevenson's translation, employing words such as "careless," "a complete failure," "an incompetent undertaking," and "amateur … at every turn."[8] William Thayer adds that the translation is "inconsistent," "introduces many errors," and is "in spots downright inane."[9]

In this regard, in cross-checking just those few Ptolemaic entries found here in my table 5, combined with about six coastal sites located in extreme southwest Canaan, I discovered no fewer than a dozen readings given by Stevenson which deviate from corresponding values found in the standard Greek editions of Ptolemy. It is also pertinent to point out that Stevenson's maps come from an early Germanus manuscript now located in the New York Public Library—the *codex Ebner* (Vat. Lat. 3810).[10] I must stress here that these Germanus Renaissance maps lack scale, grid, and proper orientation; they are consistently distorted and unreliable in shoreline allocation and configuration, and Germanus's site placements are quite generalized and often mistaken. Thomson—the widely acclaimed authority of classical studies—rightly declares that these Germanus maps "swarm with errors."[11]

In other words, Stevenson's failed translation of entirely secondary Latin sources, combined with his exclusive use of fatally flawed maps from the Renaissance period, render his work radically errant, unreliable, and almost useless for a study of classical geography in general and of Ptolemy in particular. For these reasons, I have chosen to

---

7. Edward L. Stevenson, *Claudius Ptolemy: The Geography, Based upon Greek and Latin Manuscripts and Important Late Fifteenth and Early Sixteenth Century Printed Editions* (New York: New York Public Library, 1932).

8. Aubrey Diller, review of *Claudius Ptolemy: The Geography*, by Edward Stevenson, *Isis* 22.2 (1935): 535–39.

9. William Thayer, "Ptolemy: the Geography," http://penelope.uchicago.edu/Thayer/E/Gazetteer/Periods/Roman/_Texts/Ptolemy/home.html.

10. Cf. Stevenson, *Claudius Ptolemy*, xv; note that his translation is dedicated to Donnus Nicolaus Germanus (19–21).

11. Thomson, *History of Ancient Geography*, 230.

ignore Stevenson's work here. Regrettably, Fritz employs Stevenson's English translation and one Germanus map derived ultimately from the *codex Ebner* as his principle cartographic support for the assertion that the Gulf of Aqaba/Elat was still poorly understood in the time of Ptolemy.[12] In fact, what was "poorly understood" resides in the skewed Renaissance cartographic portrayal reflected in Germanus, embraced by Stevenson, and adopted by Fritz, which stands in vivid contradistinction to the robust and remarkably accurate scholarship displayed by Ptolemy in the classical period. We still in the twenty-first century employ some of Ptolemy's basic locative system and some of the map projections he invented.

The process of making precise comparisons between Ptolemy's published values of spherical longitude and latitude and modern geodetic data, as done below for table 5, requires several technical adjustments. First, one must account for the fact that, according to Ptolemy's system, both longitudinal and latitudinal linear distances were measured in terms of the hours of a day, rather than the degrees of an arc.[13] For Ptolemy, there were sixty minutes in each degree of longitude and latitude, each minute corresponding to 1.15286 miles (1.85535 km) at zero longitude and zero latitude.[14] Thus, for example, as can be seen on table 5, Aelana village was registered by Ptolemy at 29° 15′ N (i.e., 29°, plus an additional fifteen minutes [= some 17.23 miles (27.83 km)]) north of zero latitude, and at 35° 15′ E (i.e., 35°, plus an additional fifteen minutes [= some 17.23 miles (27.83 km)]) east of zero longitude. For an exact comparison today, Ptolemy's values must be converted from minutes into decimal degrees (various computer programs that accurately render such a conversion are available from Google Earth). These conversions will appear to manifest a standard deviation of approximately 0.3′–0.5′ from Ptolemy's values, but this is

---

12. Fritz, "Lost Sea of Exodus" (2006), 232–33 [Figure 10.3]; Fritz, *Lost Sea of Exodus* (2016), 113 [Figure 8.4].

13. Ptolemy, *Geographia* 1.23 [N 1:45–47; SG 1:114–117].

14. See Vincent Virga, *Cartographia: Mapping Civilizations* (New York: Little, Brown , 2008), 20–24.

usually only a reflection of the maximal fractional variation between sixty minutes versus one hundred decimal degrees, and it therefore does not normally represent a marked deviation.

Second, in the *Geographia*, Ptolemy followed the groundbreaking work of Marinus of Tyre and adopted as his prime meridian (zero longitude line) the Fortunate/Canary Islands, whereas of course modern values are reckoned from Greenwich, England.[15] Hence, it is necessary for contemporary scholarship to subject Ptolemy's longitude E computations to an additional conversion, so as to facilitate a reasonable reconciliation with a modern geodetic grid system and to pinpoint Ptolemy's longitudinal calculations on a modern map. To illustrate, Ptolemy calculated the longitude of Aelana village at ξε° Lϛ′ (i.e., 65° 40′ E of zero longitude). A standard conversion of that registration in a modern geodetic grid system renders Ptolemy's calculation of Aelana's longitude at 35° 15′ E. Table 5 gives Ptolemaic coordinates in degrees and minutes based on this standard conversion as just described. Modern coordinates are given in the more precise degrees, minutes, and seconds.

15. See Ptolemy, *Geographia* 4.16.34 (α°); see also Dilke, *Greek and Roman Maps*, 184; J. Lennart Berggren and Alexander Jones, *Ptolemy's* Geography: *An Annotated Translation of the Theoretical Chapters* (Princeton: Princeton University Press, 2000), 11.

TABLE 5: Ptolemy's data on the Gulf of Aqaba/Elat, the Sinai Peninsula, and contiguous terrain

Ptolemaic entry[16]	Modern name	Ptolemaic citation in the *Geographia*	Ptolemaic coordinates	Modern coordinates[17]
(1) Aelana village[18] (see also #16)	'Aqaba[19]	5.17.1 (18–19)[20] [N 2:68; SG 2:576–77]	29° 15′ N[21] 35° 15′ E	29° 31′ 18″ N 35° 00′ 08″ E

---

16. Entries are arranged alphabetically.

17. Specifically, Reference System 1980 (GRS 80) and Doppler satellite images used to create a world geodetic grid system, known today as WGS 84. Since the Gulf of Aqaba/Elat is north of the equator and east of Greenwich, all listed values are positive values. Ptolemy's latitude N computations employed the equator as his standard parallel (zero latitude line). As with longitude, Ptolemy preferred to express his latitudinal values in terms of the length of a day, rather than the degrees of an arc (see page 98 above).

18. Furthermore, in his text, Ptolemy adds a short verbal description of the placement of Aelana: "The village of Aelana is situated at the farthest corner of the gulf having the same name as the gulf" [*hē de Elana kōmē kata ton mychon keimenē tou homōnymos kolpos epechei*]. Moreover, in this section (5.17.1), Ptolemy also makes reference to the Gulf of Arabia [*Arabikou kolpou*], the Gulf of Heroonpolis [*Hērōopolitēn kolpon*], and the Gulf of Elanites [*Elanitē kolpō*].

19. According to BNP 1:920, the Arabic word *'aqaba* was first attested in literature from medieval geographers, in the expression 'Aqabat 'Ayla ["the pass/lowland (>Arab, **'qab*) of Aila"], making reference to the descending route that approaches modern Aqaba from the northeast through the Wadi Yutm gorge; for similar uses of the word, see 'Aqabat Afiq, 'Aqabat Clerach, 'Aqabat al-Urqub, etc.

20. Variability among early printed editions may be observed with respect to the division of Ptolemy's work into chapters and sections, including the assignment of numbers. In this regard, it is not even clear that Ptolemy himself was responsible for this sort of classification, as it is not found in some early editions (e.g., Rome 1478; Ulm 1482). For a still useful bibliography of Ptolemy maps, see William Harris Stahl, *Ptolemy's Geography: A Select Bibliography* (New York: New York Public Library, 1953), 67–69; and for Ptolemy atlases, see 78–79.

21. My somewhat selective examination of various early printed editions of Ptolemy (e.g., Bologna 1477; Rome 1478; Ulm 1482; Florence 1482; Sylvanus 1511; Strasburg 1513; Ziegler 1532; Basel 1540; Müller 1861) makes it clear that some of the classical geographer's published values do vary from edition to edition, particularly when dealing with geographical entities located at some distance away from Alexandria (e.g., Byzantium, Babylon, Taprobane/Sri Lanka). This may be the result of copyist mistakes or just as likely of deliberate attempts on the part of later editors to improve on perceived errors in Ptolemy's original data (cf. Berggren and Jones, *Ptolemy's Geography*, 42–43). It is important to note, however, that the Red Sea data displayed here on my table from the Nobbe and the Stückelberger/Grasshoff editions are not at significant variance from the earlier printed editions of Ptolemy (e.g., Basel: Aelana village longitude 35° 38′ E; Strasburg: Aelana village latitude 29° 30′ N.; Florence: Arsinoe latitude 29° 03′ N; Rome: Eboda longitude 33° 45′ E; Ulm: Eboda longitude 34° 30′ E; Strasburg: Myos

Ptolemaic entry	Modern name	Ptolemaic citation in the *Geographia*	Ptolemaic coordinates	Modern coordinates
(2) Alexandria	Alexandria	4.5.9 (10–11) [N 1:251; SG 1:422–23]	31° 00′ N 29° 55′ E	31° 11′ 41″ N 29° 54′ 14″ E
(3) Arsinoe	Suez	4.5.14 (17) [N 1:252; SG 1:424–25]	29° 10′ N 32° 45′ E	29° 57′ 56″ N 32° 33′ 32″ E
(4) Berenike (Troglodytike)	Ras Banas	4.5.15 (28) [N 1:252; SG 1:424–25]	23° 50′ N 35° 20′ E	23° 54′ 35″ N 35° 28′ 22″ E
(5) Clysma fort	Qal'at el-Qulsum	4.5.14 (18)[22] [N 1:252; SG 1:424–25]	29° 20′ N 32° 45′ E	29° 58′ 25″ N 32° 33′ 33″ E
(5) Eboda	`Avdat	5.17.4 (10) [N 2:69; SG 2:576–77]	30° 30′ N 34° 40′ E	30° 47′ 40″ N 34° 46′ 24″ E
(6) Heroonpolis	Tell el-Maskhuta	4.5.13 (11–12) [N 1:252; SG 1.424–25]	29° 50′ N 32° 03′ E	30° 33′ 09″ N 32° 05′ 54″ E
(7) Macna	Maqna[23]	6.7.27 (17) [N 2:104; SG 2:628–29]	28° 45′ N 34° 45′ E	28° 24′ 10″ N 34° 44′ 35″ E
(8) Memphis	Mit Rahina	4.5.55 (17) [N 1:261; SG 1:436–37]	29° 50′ N 31° 15′ E	29° 51′ 40″ N 31° 15′ 15″ E

Hormos latitude 29° 50′ N). Facsimile copies of most of these early printed editions of Ptolemy can be conveniently accessed in the Newberry Library (Chicago).

22. See *BNP* 11/1:881.

23. More precisely, this entry reads "Macna and Maina." For modern Maqna, see Müller, *Geographi Graeci Minores*, map VI; Kenneth Mason, ed., *Western Arabia and the Red Sea*, Geographical Handbook Series, BR 527 (Oxford: Naval Intelligence Division, 1946), *NG* map 76 (X11); and *BAGRW* map 76 (F5); *TBA* B/V/17.2 (28.15/34.40); P. J. Parr, G. L. Harding, and J. E. Dayton, "Preliminary Survey in N. W. Arabia, 1968," *Bulletin of the Institute of Archaeology, University of London* 10 (1971): 24, 35; M. Raschke, "New Studies in Roman Commerce with the East," *ANRW* 2.9.2:875 n. 966, argues that Maqna was a port on the Gulf of Aqaba/Elat serving the large site of al-Bad'; see *BAGRW* map B/V/22.

Ptolemaic entry	Modern name	Ptolemaic citation in the *Geographia*	Ptolemaic coordinates	Modern coordinates
(9) Myos Hormos	Quseir al-Qadim	4.5.14 (20) [N 1:252; SG 1:424–25]	27° 30′ N 33° 30′ E	26° 09′ 22″ N 34° 14′ 33″ E
(10) Petra	Petra	5.17.5 (17) [N 2:69; SG 2:578–79]	30° 20′ N 35° 05′ E	30° 19′ 45″ N 35° 26′ 35″ E
(11) Pharan promontory	Ras Muhammad	5.17.1 (11–12) [N 2:68; SG 2:576–77]	28° 03′ N 34° 25′ E	27° 44′ 27″ N 34° 14′ 41″ E
(12) Pharan village[24]	Feiran	5.17.1 (16–17) [N 2:68; SG 2:576–77]	28° 40′ N 33° 25′ E	28° 42′ 14″ N 33° 38′ 02″ E
(13) Porphyry mountain	Jebel Abu Dukhan	4.5.27 (13) [N 1:255; SG 1:428–29]	26° 40′ N 32° 25′ E	27° 12′ 54″ N 33° 16′ 24″ E

---

24. Pharan is identified by Ptolemy [5.17.1 (18–19)] as a village situated deep in the Sinai Peninsula [*apo tou ektetheimenou pros tē Aigyptō peratos mechri tou kata Pharan akrōtēriou, ho epechei moiras*], and Eusebius (914/166.12-15) situated the site a journey of three days from Aila. According to Uzi Dahari, *Monastic Settlements in South Sinai in the Byzantine Period: The Archaeological Remains*, IAAR 9 (Jerusalem: Israel Antiquities Authority, 2000), 8, all of south Sinai, including Pharan, belonged to Arabia Petraea (and see Thomas, "Port Communities and the Erythraean Sea Trade," 189). Note also that in 5.17.3 (N 2:68), Ptolemy identified some of the inhabitants of Sinai as Saracene, perhaps the earliest attestation of the name "Saracens" (see also Michael O'Connor, "The Etymology of *Saracen* in Aramaic and Pre-Islamic Arabic Contexts," in *The Defence of the Roman and Byzantine East: Proceedings of a Colloquium Held at the University of Sheffield in April 1986*, ed. Philip Freeman and David Kennedy, British Institute of Archaeology at Ankara Monograph 8, BARIS 297 [Oxford: BAR, 1986], for the etymology of the word, "company/federation," and later generalized to all Arabs); see also Anastasius the Monk, in F. Nau, "Le texte grec des récits du moine Anastase sur les saints pères du Sinaï," *OC* 2 (1902): 87; and Alain Marchadour and David Neuhaus, *The Land, the Bible, and History: Toward the Land That I Will Show You* (New York: Fordham University Press, 2007), 106–7. Paran is also cited in early Christian literature, e.g., Egeria (Wilkinson, *Egeria's Travels*, 105–6); Theodosius (Paul Geyer, "Theodosii, De situ Terrae Sanctae," in *Itineraria et alia geographica*, ed. Ezio Franceschini, Robert Weber, and Paul Geyer, CCSL 175 [Turnhout: Brepols, 1965]), 123; Piacenza pilgrim (Geyer, "Theodosii," 147); Stephen of Byzantium (Augusti Meineke, *Stephan von Byzanz: Ethnika* [Graz: Akademische Drucke & Verlagsanstalt, 1958], 658). One should take note of Ptolemy's placement of Pharan and his description that the site was situated deep in the Sinai Peninsula, in contrast to the shoreline of the Germanus map; similarly, it is relevant to observe that Ptolemy differentiated between Pharan village and Pharan promontory.

Ptolemaic entry	Modern name	Ptolemaic citation in the *Geographia*	Ptolemaic coordinates	Modern coordinates
(14) Ptolemais Hormos	El-Lâhûn[25]	4.5.57 (30) [N 1:261; SG 1:438–39]	29° 20′ N 31° 05′ E	29° 14′ 14″ N 30° 58′ 13″ E
(15) Sapphirine Island	Jebel Jubal[26]	4.5.77 (12–13) [N 1:265; SG 1:443–44]	28° 00′ N 34° 15′ E	27° 38′ 51″ N 33° 48′ 12″ E
(16) Turn of the Aelanites Gulf[27] (see also #1)	Head of the Gulf of Aqaba	5.17.1 (14–15); 5.17.1 (10–13) [N 2:68; SG 2:576–77]	29° 00′ N 35° 25′ E	29° 33′ 05″ N 34° 57′ 12″ E

The graphics of Ptolemy's work follows. Map 7a attempts to plot Ptolemy's registered values spatially as they appear in table 5. His

25. See John Baines and Jaromir Málek, *Atlas of Ancient Egypt* (New York: Facts On File, 1980), 41, 43, 121.

26. Refer to Mason, *Western Arabia*, 82 for Jebel Jubal and the Strait of Jubal.

27. Ptolemy also makes mention of the "Leanites Gulf" [6.7.18 (1), *Leanitēs kolpos*], but both his context and his locational coordinates make clear the fact that he has another body of water in view. There in context, Ptolemy is delineating features of his sixth map of Asia (not his fourth map of Asia), starting with the coastal regions and peoples of Arabia Felix and concluding with a discussion of the towns and villages situated in the interior of the peninsula. His discussion of the maritime coast (*paralios*) advances essentially in a counterclockwise direction, beginning at the northern terminus of the Arabian Gulf near the Elanites Bay and ending in the northern reaches of the Persian Gulf. Along the way, Ptolemy enumerates coastal entities such as Modiana [6.7.2 (17)], Hippos village [6.7.2 (19)], Phoinikon village [6.7.3 (20)], Raunathou village [6.7.3 (21)], the Thamyditai people [6.7.4 (25)], the Sidenoi people [6.7.4 (26)], the Darae people [6.7.4 (27)], the Banoubaroi people [6.7.4 (1)], the Arsai people [6.7.4 (2)], the Kinaidokolpitai region [6.7.5; for all of these, refer to *BAGRW* map 83], and the Kassanita region [6.7.6; see Meineke, *Stephan von Byzanz*, 365]. Continuing, Ptolemy then mentions arriving at *Erythras thalassēs meta ta stena* [6.7.8 (26)], presumably the Strait of Bab el-Mandab, after which he proceeds to register more than thirty-five places, largely unknown but all bearing longitudinal coordinates that are fairly consistent with the southern coast of the Arabian Peninsula. At the conclusion of that list, Ptolemy then records the entry "the Strait of the Persian Gulf" (*en tois stenois tou Persikou kolpou*) [6.7.12 (11); cf. 6.7.14 (4–5)]. From that point, Ptolemy makes mention of numerous locations along the Arabian coast of the Persian Gulf, including the Mykoi people [6.7.14 (7); see *BAGRW* map 95 inset], the town of Gerrha [6.7.16 (19); see *BAGRW* map 95 (A3); *TBA* map B/V/3, B/V/4], the Laenitae people [6.7.18 (28)], and finally the Leanites Gulf [6.7.18 (1)]. Beyond context, Ptolemy's grid coordinates for the "Leanites Gulf" [48° 40′ longitude E; 27° 00′ latitude N] place it near the Arabian coast of the Persian Gulf, between modern Kuwait and Bahrain, more than 12° E of the Gulf of Aqaba/ Elat (and see its placement on Ptolemy's sixth map of Asia).

values and the corresponding modern data for the same sites are represented with bullets according to the legend on the map. It is pertinent to observe how a number of Ptolemy's port city registrations align with substantial precision to modern coastlines. It is also relevant in this context to notice that the geographer considered the latitude N coordinate for Aelana village (29° 15′, at the head of the Gulf of Aqaba/Elat) to be basically parallel with those of Arsinoe/Suez (29° 10′) and Clysma Fort (29° 20′, at the head of the Gulf of Suez). At the same time, it is helpful to make a comparison of Ptolemy's longitude E for Aelana village and for Arsinoe (35° 15′ E vs. 32° 45′ E), or some 2.5° (roughly 173 miles [278 km]) between the heads of the two gulfs (the modern intermediate air distance is 159 miles [256 km]). Here is statistical evidence to demonstrate Ptolemy's awareness of the approximate location, configuration, and dimension of the Gulf of Aqaba/Elat.

On map 7b, Germanus's coastal delineations as they appear on the illustrative map selected by Fritz are depicted, both for the Red Sea and for the southeast extremity of the Mediterranean. One can immediately notice how the Renaissance shorelines are radically different from modern shorelines. One can also observe an almost total lack of spatial correspondence between Ptolemy's site placements and Germanus's shoreline delineations. A number of Ptolemy's registrations (and modern sites) would lie inundated according to the Germanus shoreline configurations (e.g., Pharan village; Pharan promontory; Sapphirine Island; Myos Hormos; Berenike). Finally, one notices that the Germanus shoreline at the point of intersecting the Gulf of Aqaba/Elat is not near Ptolemy's registration of Aelana village and the Turn of the Aelanites Gulf.

Maps 7a and 7b plot all of Ptolemy's recorded latitudinal and longitudinal registrations relating to the Gulf of Aqaba/Elat and the Sinai Peninsula, some sixteen entries. If one considers all sixteen latitude N values found on the maps—after a standard conversion, and disregarding any possible fractional variation (which would likely bring his results into closer alignment with modern data; see page 98 above)—the average variance between Ptolemy values and modern geodetic data is 25.36 minutes (i.e., 29.21 miles [47.12 km]).[28] Taking the same purview of his sixteen longitudinal E readings, the average variance between Ptolemy and geodetic data is 15.56 minutes (i.e., 18.08 miles [29.134 km]). I believe this demonstrates that Ptolemy's spherically calculated values consistently possess reasonable, trustworthy credibility.

To be sure, Ptolemy's work is not flawless and comes with certain caveats. His grid calculations go beyond the bounds of the Roman Empire (e.g., southern Africa; India; even into the Gulf of Thailand [Magnus Sinus]), into largely uncharted zones where his values are in error by a considerable measure. He imprecisely calculated the total length of the Mediterranean Sea; his adoption of the Fortunate/Canary Islands as his prime meridian (see page 99 above), even after being subjected to a standard conversion and brought into conformity with Greenwich, still lacks the pinpoint precision of a single, fixed anchor city, and this offers the potential for slightly affecting some of his longitude E values.

Moreover, it is also true that Ptolemy benefited from an accumulated bank of geographical data that had earlier been discovered or retrieved by others and was available to him in Alexandria (e.g., from

---

28. The average differential is reduced to 22.20 miles (35.73 km) if one considers his Myos Hormos value to be an outlier. The early Ptolemies established two significant harbors on the Gulf of Arabia: Berenike (Trogodytike) and Myos Hormos. The location of Berenike (see map 7a) has long been established in classical scholarship. On the other hand, the location of the port of Myos Hormos has until very recently been in dispute. One proposed site lay just to the north of modern Hurghada, at the port of Abu Sha'ar—almost pinpointed by Ptolemy's bullet for Myos Hormos on map 7a (for this same [mis]placement of Myos Hormos on a very recent map of the Red Sea in the classical period, see Kerkeslager, "Jewish Pilgrimage," 105). The other proposal for the site of Myos Hormos lay about ninety-nine miles (160 km) to the south, at modern Quseir al-Qudim (the modern location plotted on map 7a). This latter site has only recently been confirmed as the port of ancient Myos Hormos (see, e.g., Lucy Blue, "Locating the Harbour: Myos Hormos/Quseir al-Qadim; a Roman and Islamic Port on the Red Sea Coast of Egypt," *IJNA* 36.2 [2007]: 265–81). Given the close proximity of Ptolemy's registration to Abu Sha'ar, and his otherwise characteristic variance in the placement of sites along the shoreline of the Gulf of Aqaba/Elat, it seems that Ptolemy may have been following what is now known to have been an incorrect locational tradition. Thus it is reasonable to consider this value as an outlier.

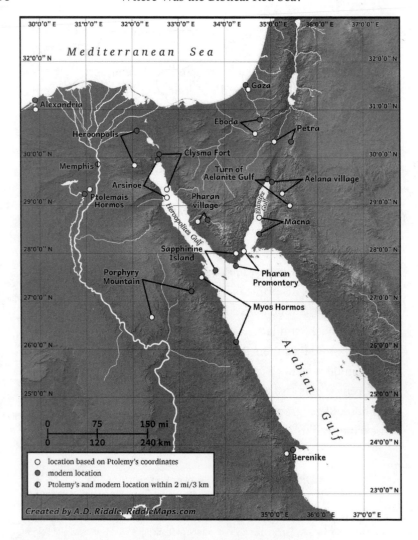

MAP 7A: **Ptolemy's locations in the Sinai region**

This map displays latitude/longitude of cities in the Sinai, near the Gulf of Aqaba/Elat, and contiguous terrain based on Ptolemy's coordinates

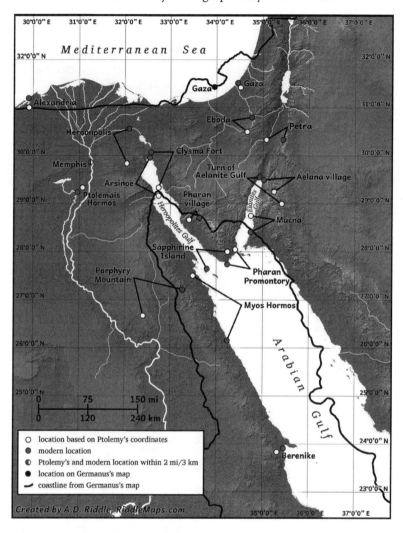

MAP 7B: **Ptolemy's locations in the Sinai region with Germanus's coastlines**

This map displays latitude/longitude of cities in the Sinai, near the Gulf of Aqaba/ Elat, and contiguous terrain based on Ptolemy's coordinates and with Germanus's coastlines marked

the calculations of earlier astronomers or the notes of earlier explor-
ers; from the extensive work of Alexandrian bematists [professional
walkers specially trained to measure distance by counting their steps];
from long-distance trading networks across the entire Roman world
and including Chinese merchants exporting silk to parts of Europe;
from Roman land surveyors; from the extensive paved Roman road
system; from thousands of milestones; and from an abundant array
of recorded itineraries).

Nevertheless, Ptolemy's novel, highly technical introduction of
spherical latitude and longitude, and the creation of a formal grid
system into this mix, provided for the first time a comprehensive
way for cartographers to plot direction and linear distance on a map,
along with scale and orientation, and in particular intelligently to
portray geographical data relating to a spherical planet onto a flat
surface. This watershed achievement was truly a game changer for
classical geography in particular and even for geography in general.
Ronald Abler, John Adams, and Peter Gould have rightly commented,
"much of our geography [today] is a series of footnotes to Ptolemy."[29]

Fritz's summary dismissal of Ptolemy's geographic acumen and
cartographic knowledge, based on this one Germanus map, is rather
misguided and misinformed. One must direct the map's self-evident
deficiencies to Germanus, not Ptolemy, since the map in question is
a Renaissance-period map and specifically a Germanus map, not a
Ptolemy map (see page 104–5). True, the map can be identified today
as a "Ptolemy Asia IV" map, but such wording in the geographic discipline was never intended to identify Ptolemy as the map's author/cre-
ator. Rather, this wording merely indicates that the map design derives
ultimately from one of the several theoretical projection grid systems
for terrestrial representation introduced by Ptolemy and contained
in his *Geographia*.[30] Christopher Columbus—a near contemporary

---

29. Abler, Adams, and Gould, *Spatial Organization*, 64.

30. Dilke, "Culmination of Greek Cartography," 185; Ptolemy's *Geographia* sets forth several
different portrayal systems, perhaps as many as four grid systems. For a very helpful discussion and representation of Ptolemy maps, coming from either the Renaissance period or even

of Germanus—when preparing to sail west from Spain to India, also employed a Ptolemy map,[31] once again referencing Ptolemy's conceptual cartographic framework for treating spherical latitude and longitude on a flat surface, not a map specimen actually created by the great classical geographer. In point of fact, professional mapmakers today continue to debate the question of whether or not Ptolemy ever actually produced a single map personally, and in any case no such maps are known to be extant.[32] Moreover, Ptolemy understandably did not normally supply grid coordinates for shoreline configurations in the *Geographia,* and certainly none are given for the Red Sea or for the Sinai.

Beyond this one map, and more generally in regard to his methodology, Fritz relies entirely on the many glaring geographical deficiencies found in Renaissance-era maps and reflected in contemporary Renaissance authors to underscore his hypothesis two, that geographical knowledge of the Gulf of Aqaba/Elat was materially absent throughout the classical period.[33] Hundreds of such Renaissance map specimens exist (and Fritz has included some forty images in his most recent work), and these maps customarily lack scale, grid, and direct orientation, and they often show distorted shorelines in a scalloped-like design, bearing little resemblance to reality (see map 8).

portrayed in modern times, see Berggren and Jones, *Ptolemy's* Geography, pls. 1–6, maps 1–8b. Fritz's fundamental misunderstanding of what it means in the discipline to identify a Ptolemy map is unmistakably illustrated in a recent post on his website. There he states that his figure 1 (a Renaissance-era map) "is based on the c. 150 AD work of the Greek Geographer Ptolemy, who compiled the geographical knowledge of the 2nd-century AD Roman Empire" (https://ancientexodus.com/proof-of-mount-sinai-in-arabia/).

31. Despite what George Santayana declares in his poem, "Faith," that Columbus sailed only with a "map" that could be deciphered in the skies. A Ptolemy map was likely procured by Columbus's brother Bartholomew, who was himself a professional geographer and who accompanied Christopher on the 1492 mission.

32. For a helpful discussion, consult Alexander Jones, "Ptolemy's Geography: Mapmaking and the Scientific Enterprise," in *Ancient Perspectives: Maps and Their Place in Mesopotamia, Egypt, Greece and Rome,* ed. Richard J. A. Talbert (Chicago: University of Chicago Press, 2012), 122–25, and see the bibliography cited there.

33. See Fritz, "Lost Sea of Exodus" (2006), 169 (12.4.3) for a clear methodological statement in this regard.

MAP 8: **Map of Ptolemy: Asia IV**

"Map of Ptolemy: Asia IV–Syria, Coele-Syria, Palestina, Arabia Petraea, Arabia Deserta, Mesopotamia, Babylonia"; 1460; New York Public Library; Manuscript from Nicolas Germanus

Based on a distorted shoreline of the Gulf of Aqaba/Elat appearing on a "Ptolemy" map produced by the early Renaissance cartographer Nicolas Germanus, Fritz argues that the Gulf of Aqaba/Elat was "poorly understood" in the classical period (*Lost Sea of the Exodus* [2016], 113). However, the projection protocols found in Ptolemy's *Geographia* include latitudinal and longitudinal coordinates useful primarily in plotting individual towns and cities. The *Geographia* may sometimes also include coordinates for islands, mountains, rivers, and provinces, but in all of these latter categories, one must bear in mind that Ptolemy's placements denote a particular point in latitude/ longitude, not the entire perimeter of an island or a province, nor the entire range of a mountain, nor the entire course of a river. And with respect to the Gulf of Aqaba/ Elat or the Sinai, Ptolemy never includes linear data having to do with shorelines. Accordingly, the myriad of cartographic errors or distortions in islands, mountains, rivers, provinces, and especially shorelines manifested on a Germanus's map cannot logically be ascribed to Ptolemy. Furthermore, as clearly demonstrated on the "Ptolemy" map seen here, glaring distortion of early Renaissance shorelines can be seen across the entire eastern Mediterranean, in areas categorically well-known and understood in the classical period. Relevant in this regard are the striking distortions around Gaza or, farther north, the highly erratic protrusion near Joppa; and see especially the entire stretch of radically distorted shoreline in Lebanon and western Syria—at an even greater scale of distortion than represented at the Gulf of Aqaba/Elat—from Byblos the entire way north to Rhosos, a coastal town north of Antioch. Moreover, the false simplicity of the Cilician shoreline, along southern Asia Minor, is also noteworthy in this regard. The same is true for islands, as illustrated by the location, shoreline, and bloated size of Cyprus. Geographic distortion may also easily be seen with mountains. Note, for example, how the Lebanon mountains are set north (not west) of the Anti-Lebanon range, and both are displayed essentially on an east-west axis (instead of the actual north-south axis they both manifest). The same kind of distortion obtains with rivers on the map, clearly illustrated with the course of the Orontes River, but seen even more clearly with the wildly tentacle-like flow of both the Tigris and the Euphrates Rivers, finally joining several hundred miles north of the Persian Gulf, with only the Tigris flowing as far south as the Gulf. Data on a Germanus's map that actually derive from Ptolemy's *Geographia* relate primarily to the coordinate placement of cities, and this grid information is generally regarded to have a reasonable level of trustworthy geographical accuracy

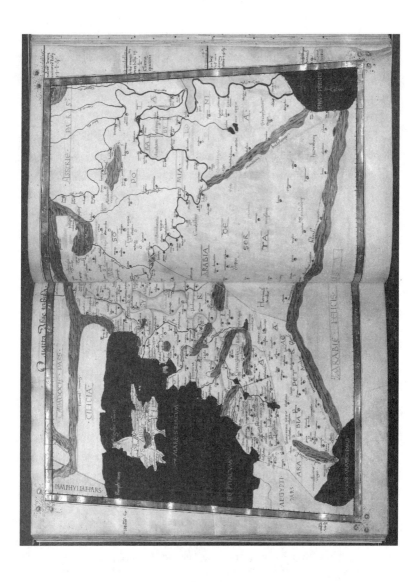

This kind of misrepresentation is true generally of these maps on a much broader areal scale, far beyond the immediate environs of the Gulf of Aqaba/Elat.[34] Fritz, however, has tended to focus more narrowly just on the spatial deficiencies as they are portrayed in and around that immediate geography. From this he deduces, fallaciously in my judgment and irrefutably out of alignment with the discipline, that the same spatial ignorance and the same geographical deficiencies observed on Renaissance maps must also have obtained in earlier periods, including and especially in the classical period. However, all of these maps date more than one thousand years after Ptolemy, and more than fifteen hundred years after the LXX Pentateuch was translated in Alexandria. Whatever deficiencies these maps manifest, and they are myriad, these must be ascribed to the level of knowledge (or ignorance) that prevailed at the time they were executed. They neither embody nor reflect in any way the level of accumulated scholarly geographic knowledge as it had come to exist in the classical world.

What amounts to a loss of classical geographic literacy and the subsequent accumulation of woefully deficient Renaissance-era maps must be ascribed to other intermediate causes and forces. Thus, for example, as has been abundantly and unequivocally demonstrated in literature addressing the history of cartography, with the emergence of Christianity as a dominant force within the Roman Empire, there followed a dramatic decline of classical scientific methodology within established religion. Investigative inquiry in a number of the sciences, including geography and cartography, came to be regarded

---

34. An illustration of this point can be found in Fritz (*Lost Sea of Exodus* [2016], 206, fig. 14.2, also identified as a Ptolemy map). Here, e.g., it is easy to observe the scalloped shoreline of the eastern Mediterranean, including a rump in the southeastern corner, the shape, length and the tentacle-like nature of the Abana and Jordan rivers, a mysterious east-west mountain range shown south of Damascus, the shape and location of the Dead Sea, etc. Renaissance-era maps manifest the same distortions throughout most of the Mediterranean world, across Asia Minor, much of Europe, and southern Asia (consult, e.g., Kenneth Nebenzahl, *Maps of the Holy Land: Images of Terra Sancta through Two Millennia* [New York: Abbeville Press, 1986], 20–23, 31, 44–45, 58–59, 70–71, 78–79, 86–87, 124–25, 129), and the mysterious shoreline delineations are by no means limited to the immediate geography of the Gulf of Aqaba/Elat.

as possibly pagan and certainly irrelevant.[35] As Kenneth Nebenzahl has rightly observed, early Christian mapmakers "didn't bother with the latitude of the next city when paradise was out there waiting to be mapped in all its glory."[36]

In this regard, it is necessary to acknowledge a dual tendency in early Christian exegesis that was to prove fatal to scientific cartography for at least a millennium. First, the scholarly cartographic advances of classical scientists such as Ptolemy, and the promising site identification methodologies represented, for example, by the work of Eusebius, became suffocated by established ecclesiastical tradition. Site placement and identification for the sake of learning gave way to identification as a stimulus to religious sentiment, and not until the time of Gerhard Kremer (Mercator, c. 1540) were meridians and parallels scientifically reintroduced into cartography, and not until the time of Napoleon (c. 1798) and Edward Robinson (c. 1840) were scientific surveys of the Holy Land fully resumed.

Second, certain biblical affirmations were converted into a veritable dogma of the church, or traditions arose amid inferences derived from early Christian pilgrims; in either case, these were literally put into practice by medieval Christian cartographers. Accordingly, early Christian maps are more ecclesiastic than cartographic, more symbolic than realistic, more art than science. They reflect Christian dogma more than observed fact; they are more preoccupied with propagating theology than either geography or cartography. These maps lack scale or grid, and they frequently show direction incorrectly or even variably on one and the same map, repudiating as they consistently do the cartographic framework that had been painstakingly worked out by Eratosthenes and Ptolemy and their classical associates.

---

35. A very helpful bibliographic springboard into the relevant literature addressing the relationship between the early church and science may be found in David C. Lindberg, "Science and the Early Christian Church," *Isis* 74 (1983): 509–30. See also David C. Lindberg and Ronald L. Numbers, eds., *When Science and Christianity Meet* (Chicago: University of Chicago Press, 2003). Refer most recently to Catherine Nixey, *The Darkening Age: The Christian Destruction of the Classical World* (Boston: Houghton Mifflin Harcourt, 2018).

36. Nebenzahl, *Maps of the Holy Land*, 13.

MAP 9: **Anglo-Saxon map**

Anglo-Saxon Cotton Collection Map of the World (c. 995–1050; British Museum; Manuscript discovered as part of the sixteenth century collection of Robert Cotton, which formed the nucleus of the British Library)

Thought to have been the work of an Irish scholar-monk, the "Anglo-Saxon" map (as it has come to be known, because some of the writing is in Anglo-Saxon)—like most T-O maps (which depict the world as a circle with a T inside; see page 115)—is oriented to east, in this case picturing the world from India and Sri Lanka (shown at the top edge, center) as far west as the Pillars of Hercules and the passageway to the Atlantic Ocean (bottom edge, center). The darkened area dominating the west-central portion of the map is the Mediterranean Sea, badly misshapen and mis-sized. The Nile River appears as a dark ribbon along the right side of the map, strangely flowing westward and then bending towards the north, and finally breaking into three distributaries and entering the southeast corner of the Mediterranean.

Like other T-O maps, three continents are delineated (Asia, east of the Mediterranean; Europe, north of the Mediterranean; and Africa, south of the Mediterranean), surrounded by a circumfluent ocean, with scalloped-like, erratic shore-lines. Featured just south of center and east of the Mediterranean is Jerusalem, sur-rounded by walls and a tower. A number of Roman provincial names appear on the map, especially across Asia Minor (left-center, south of the crescent-shaped, dark-ened interior sea [Black Sea]). The darkened area to the northeast of the Black Sea is the Caspian Sea (pictured with two islands), bloated and mistakenly shown opening into the circumfluent ocean. Adjacent to this opening, on the west side, one can see depicted the land of Gog and Magog, situated inside a containment wall. To the south of Asia Minor, and for the first time on a world map, the territory of Israel's twelve tribes appears, depicted mostly in rectangular shape, within straight painted lines (nine tribes are named). Notice how much area of the world is taken up by Israel's tribes. Snaking its way through the tribes, the Jordan River originates near the biblical site of Caesarea Philippi and flows southward into the Dead Sea. Mt. Sinai and Mt. Ararat, including a three-storey Noah's ark, are portrayed, as is a scattering of biblical towns, including such places as Jericho, Bethlehem, Antioch, Babylon, Rome, and Tarshish.

MAP 10: **Psalter map**

Psalter Map of the World (c. 1225–1265; British Museum; Map appended to a Latin manuscript of the Book of Psalms)

One of the most ornate and detailed T-O maps, the Psalter map in typical fashion is oriented to the east and is transparently removed from the cartographic science of the classical culture. In this case, a circular world is depicted from Paradise (portrayed as a walled circle at the easternmost extremity) west as far as the entrance to the Atlantic Ocean. Here again the world is pictured surrounded by a circumfluent ocean, and a distorted Mediterranean Sea divides the continents of Europe (north of the sea) and Africa, and it also effectively partitions off the continent of Asia (the entire eastern part of the circle). The Nile Delta appears distinctly, with the river's seven distributaries emptying into the southeastern corner of the Mediterranean. Following medieval tradition, Jerusalem figures prominently at dead center on the map, an epicenter emphasized by its precise location and its large and conspicuous painted circle. Other biblical motifs represented here include the ark of Noah (perched atop Mt. Ararat, northeast of Jerusalem, about midway to the outer ocean), the "barns of Joseph" (cf. Gen 41:34–36; situated southeast of Jerusalem), and especially the garden of Eden. In this instance the circle at the top of the map displays the faces of Adam and Eve, and five rivers radiate from that idyllic scenery (the Ganges River is mistakenly included). Like the Anglo-Saxon map, a barrier wall along the northeast portion of the map effectively shuts in and constrains the forces of Gog and Magog, thought in medieval tradition to overrun the world on the day of judgment. The map likewise depicts the containment of fourteen monstrous races in southernmost Africa, related in some way to the various people groups of Islam. Sites of the biblical world are represented, such as Bethlehem, Antioch, Babylon, Constantinople, Rome, and Alexandria.

Grossly distorted at many places and sometimes exaggerated as is the Psalter map, the "theological geography" of the medieval world is most plainly reflected at the very top of the image, where Jesus Christ, flanked by two angels swinging censers, is shown crushing the heads of two dragons (at the lower extremity of the map) and presiding over the whole world on the final day of judgment.

A scattering of early Christian and medieval maps seek to deny on biblical grounds that the earth was a sphere or that human beings inhabited the southern hemisphere, which was thought to be hell (cf. Dante's *Inferno*). Some maps seek to show the existence of other races not descended from the sons of Adam (e.g., the forces of Gog and Magog in the north and the diabolical forces of Islam in the south). Other maps elaborate graphically upon biblical themes: the plot of ground where Adam was created; the location of paradise and the rivers of the garden; the location of Noah's ark and the three known continents linked to the three sons of Noah and their descendants; the travels of the Israelites through Sinai; the dream of Daniel and the four beasts; the place where wood for the cross was obtained; and certain myths relating to the Sea of Galilee, the Dead Sea, and Sodom and Gomorrah. Oftentimes, these maps allot as much as 20 percent to 25 percent of the land mass of the entire world to a portrayal of the Holy Land.

The work of Isidore of Seville (c. 600), archbishop of Seville and head of the church in Spain, is seminal in this regard. Isidore amassed an unparalleled fund of secular and ecclesiastical knowledge, from which he compiled an encyclopedia known as the *Etymologies*. Scholars of the history of the early church believe that, next to the Vulgate, the *Etymologies* was the most commonly consulted volume throughout the Early Middle Ages.[37] Included in the *Etymologies* is Isidore's geographical schema of the world: a circular disc surrounded by water (based on Isa 40:22, "the circle of the earth;" cf. Job 26:10; Prov 8:27). Known as the "T-O map" (*orbis terrarum*, "the whole earth," such maps are also known today as *mappae mundi*),[38] this became the most common shape of the medieval world, and more

---

37. E.g., this is the assessment of Isidore's influence offered by Kenneth Scott Latourette, *A History of Christianity* (New York: Harper and Row, 1953), 341.

38. Consult, e.g., Peter Whitfield, *The Image of the World: 20 Centuries of World Maps* (London: British Library, 1994); Brigitte Englisch, *Ordo orbis terrae: Die Weltsicht in den Mappae mundi des frühen und hohen Mittelalters* (Berlin: Akademie, 2002), 38, 47, 49, 111, 130, 136, 196, 217, 221, 246, 261, 287, 299, 304, 312, 318, 345, 365, 391, 401, 422, 440, 457, 474, 477, and esp. 566–655.

than six hundred T-O map specimens survive to the present. The most common T-O template is oriented to the east and shows the earth divided into three continents, peopled by the three sons of Noah: Shem (associated with and often prominently displayed on the continent of Asia, the largest share to reflect his primogeniture), Ham (associated with Africa), and Japheth (associated with Europe). Another permutation of the T-O map is known today as a "tau-cross" map, which was designed to superimpose the passion of Christ upon the whole world.

Adaptations of the T-O map design wrought by Christian imagination rather than cartographic science become playful at times, and see in this regard the ornately decorated Mansel c. 1459 map ("La Fleur des Histories")[39]; in another such specimen (1580), the world is depicted as a three-leaf clover, with Jerusalem pictured at dead center (cf. Ezek 5:5, Jerusalem is set at the navel of the nations). I have discovered early Christian maps that picture the world in the shape of a heart, a double-eagle, a *fleur-de-lis*, a mandorla, a square, or an almond (supposedly to depict Noah's ark).[40]

Early post-Constantinian Christianity engaged directly with the classical world, and especially with its psyche, with its arts, and with its sciences. However, all knowledge, so the church now contended, was to be found in the Holy Scriptures, not in human reason or observation. As a result, this engagement soon became adversarial, even tempestuous, across virtually all aspects of culture and life. In the process, classical temples, shrines, and altars were razed; statues and exquisite sculptures were mutilated or crushed to powder; works of art were demolished; literature of all sorts was obliterated; and even the library at Alexandria was destroyed. Laws were created or changed, and schools were transformed or closed. Classical culture was entirely recast with a distinctly Christian face.

---

39. For an image of this map, see Beitzel, "Exegesis, Dogmatics, and Cartography," 12.

40. See Beitzel, "Exegesis, Dogmatics and Cartography" 8–21, and see various maps depicted there.

MAP 11: **Three-leaf clover map**

Bünting Clover Leaf Map of the World (1581; Eran Laor Cartographic Collection, Jerusalem; Published as part of Heinrich Bünting, *Itinerarium Sacrae Scripturae*)

An adaptation of the T-O map design is seen in this three-leaf clover map created by a German Protestant pastor, Heinrich Bünting. Oriented to north, this map again schematically presents the three continents of the world surrounded by water (Europe; Africa; Asia), here in the shape of a clover leaf, corresponding to the areas settled by the three sons of Noah. In this case, however, Bünting includes the novel idea of a fourth continent, pictured and labeled in the lower left corner: "America, Die Neue Welt" (America had been discovered some ninety years before this map was released). Once again symbolic design triumphs over geographical accuracy on this map: the city of Jerusalem is shown at the intersection of all three continents, at dead center on the map, and enormously enlarged (a banner example of the cartographic concept of heterogeneous space). Herod's Temple in Jerusalem is depicted, surrounded by Renaissance-style buildings and ramparts. Also pictured just outside the city is a hill, on which three crosses are clearly visible. Jerusalem's global centrality is also reflected in various illustrations of cities on the three continents, including a (sometimes mistaken) listing of the mileage from that city to Jerusalem (e.g., Rome—382; Alexandria—72; Damascus—40; Haran—110; Babylon—170). Between the continents of Asia and Africa, the Red Sea figures prominently on the map, both by way of its exaggerated space allotment and by way of being painted red (it may be of interest that this German Protestant pastor does not use Luther's *Schilfmeer* ["sea of reeds," Exod 15:22] in this regard).

At the time, this was largely perceived as a struggle between good and evil, between the forces of light and the forces of darkness, between God and the gods. And Christianity won! In consequence, however, early Christian maps and their controlling, underlying ideology effectively extinguished classical cartographic science as it had come to exist through the achievements of Eratosthenes and Ptolemy. At the same time, these maps of early Christianity ought to serve even today as a reminder of the harm that inevitably derives when extra-scientific ecclesiastical dogma that seeks to provide warrant for personal belief systems or sectarian creeds is allowed to substitute for an authentically scientific epistemological enterprise.

CONCLUSION

The cumulative weight of well-established scholarship in two separate professional disciplines bears heavily upon the work of Fritz. It seems unavoidable not to conclude that with his hypothesis one, Fritz is fundamentally out of step with standard, conventional biblical scholarship, and with his hypothesis two, he is likewise most certainly out of alignment with the discipline of geographical scholarship.

According to Fritz's hypothesis one, all citations of Hebrew *yam sûf* must *solely and exclusively designate* the modern Gulf of Aqaba/ Elat. It has been my effort here to provide both exegetical and documentary evidence showing this hypothesis to be idiosyncratic and highly doubtful. The hypothesis also flounders in that it largely lacks a substantive, objective evidentiary foundation, and for the most part it stands in polar opposition to both historic and contemporary scholarship across a very wide biblical and theological spectrum within the discipline.

According to his hypothesis two, all classical citations of *erythra thalassa//mare rubrum* must *specifically and invariably exclude* the Gulf of Aqaba/Elat, because in his view this body of water was materially absent from geographical knowledge and awareness throughout the classical period, as evidenced in the lack of classical documentary references to the water body and as reflected even later in Renaissance-era cartographic efforts. In this instance, I have endeavored to provide primary evidence from across the classical world, including specifically from the city of Alexandria, that conclusively demonstrates a keen scientific awareness that the Gulf of Aqaba/Elat was part of *erythra thalassa//mare rubrum* by the time Jewish scholars in that city translated the Hebrew Pentateuch into Greek. Most assuredly, the Gulf of Aqaba/Elat was in no sense lost in the Greco-Roman world. I would also contend that his two foundational and quintessential hypotheses cast their long and defining shadow over much of the related discussions in the work of Fritz.

Many salient implications derive from these evidentiary observations, but perhaps the most fundamental and significant for biblical studies include the following: (1) it is highly doubtful that the Israelite exodus from Egypt occurred at some place in the Gulf of Aqaba/Elat, hundreds of miles away from Egypt; and (2) it is baseless and indefensible to propose to locate Mt. Sinai in Saudi Arabia, to the east of the Gulf of Aqaba/Elat, based on a presumed Gulf of Aqaba/Elat exodus crossing point and/or on the geographical argumentation found in the work of Fritz. His study offers numerous, ancillary discussions and illustrations for his viewpoint that ultimately derive from and depend on the integrity of his two controlling hypotheses, none of which can retain cogency if the foundational hypothesis on which they rest has been shown to evoke the greatest doubt and/or to be factually erroneous.

Wherever the people of Israel miraculously crossed the Red Sea, or wherever Mt. Sinai is to be located, I would contend a so-called Gulf of Aqaba/Elat exodus hypothesis or a purported Mt. Sinai in Saudi Arabia hypothesis cannot on this basis withstand the scrutiny of the biblical, classical, and early cartographically related traditions presented here.

BIBLIOGRAPHY

Aalders, G. Charles. *Genesis*. Grand Rapids: Zondervan, 1981.

Abler, Ronald R., John S. Adams, and Peter Gould. *Spatial Organization: The Geographer's View of the World*. Englewood Cliffs, NJ: Prentice-Hall, 1971.

Ackroyd, Peter. *The First Book of Samuel*. CBC. Cambridge: Cambridge University Press, 1971.

Aharoni, Yohanan. *The Land of the Bible: A Historical Geography*. Philadelphia; Westminster, 1979.

Allen, Leslie. C. *The Books of Joel, Obadiah, Jonah and Micah*. NICOT. Grand Rapids: Eerdmans, 1976.

Alt, Albrecht. "Studien aus dem Deutschen evang. Institut für Altertumswissenschaft in Jerusalem: Der südliche Endabschnitt der römischen Strasse von Bostra nach Aila." *ZDPV* 59 (1936): 92–111.

Amigues, Suzanne. "Anaxikrates' Expedition to Western Arabia." Pages 189–95 in *A Gateway from the Eastern Mediterranean to India: The Red Sea in Antiquity*. Edited by Marie-Françoise Boussac and Jean-François Salles. New Delhi: Manohar, 2005.

Atlas of Israel: Cartography, Physical and Human Geography. 3rd ed. Tel Aviv: Survey of Israel, 1985.

Auld, A. Graeme. *I & II Samuel: A Commentary*. OTL. Louisville: Westminster John Knox, 2011.

Avi-Yonah, Michael. *The Holy Land from the Persian to the Arab Conquests: A Historical Geography*. Grand Rapids: Baker, 1966.

———. *The Madaba Mosaic Map*. Jerusalem: Israel Exploration Society, 1954.

Bailey, Lloyd R. *Leviticus–Numbers*. SHBC 3. Macon, GA: Smyth & Helwys, 2005.

Baines, John, and Jaromir Málek. *Atlas of Ancient Egypt*. New York: Facts On File, 1980.

Baldwin, Joyce. *1 and 2 Samuel*. TOTC. Downers Grove, IL: InterVarsity Press, 1988.

Baly, Denis. *The Geography of the Bible*. 2nd ed. New York: Harper & Row, 1974.

Bamberger, S., ed. *Raschis Pentateuchkommentar = Rashi ʾal ha-Torah*. Hamburg: Kramer, 1928.

Batto, Bernard F. "Mythic Dimensions of the Exodus Tradition." Pages 187–95 in *Israel's Exodus in Transdisciplinary Perspective: Text, Archaeology, Culture, and Geoscience*. Edited by Thomas E. Levy, Thomas Schneider, and William H. C. Propp. New York: Springer, 2015.

———. "The Reed Sea: *Requiescat in Pace*." *JBL* 102 (1983): 27–35.

Bauzou, Thomas. "A Finibus Syriae: Recherches sur les routes des frontièrs orientales de l'Empire Romain." 3 vols. PhD diss., Université de Paris I, Institut d'Art et d'Archéologie, 1989.

———. "La *via nova* en Arabie. Le secteur nord, de Bostra à Philadelphie." Pages 101–255 in *Fouilles de Khirbet es-Samra en Jordanie I*. Edited by J.-B. Humbert and A. Desreumaux. Bibliothèque de l'antiquité tardive. Turnhout: Brepols, 1998.

———. "Les voies de communications dans le Hauran à l'époque romaine." Pages 137–65 in *Hauran I: recherches archéologiques sur la Syrie du Sud à l'époque hellénistique et romaine*. Edited by J.-M. Dentzer. Paris: P. Geuthner, 1985.

———. "Les voies romaines entre Damas et Amman." Pages 292–300 in *Géographie historique au Proche-Orient (Syrie, Phénicie, Arabie, grecques, romaines, byzantines): Actes de la Table*

Ronde de Valbonne, 16–18 septembre 1985. Edited by Pierre-Louis Gatier, Bruno Helly, and Jean-Paul Rey-Coquais. Notes et monographies techniques, Centre de recherches archéologiques 23. Paris: Éditions du Centre National de la Recherché Scientifique, 1990.

Beegle, Dewey M. "Moses (Person): Old Testament." *ABD* 4:909–18.

Ben David, Chaim. "Milestones near Roman Army Installations in Desert Areas in the Provinces of Palaestina and Arabia." Pages 132–46 in *Roman Roads: New Evidence—New Perspectives.* Edited by Anne Kolb. Berlin: De Gruyter, 2019.

Beitzel, Barry J. "Exegesis, Dogmatics and Cartography: A Strange Alchemy in Earlier Church Traditions." *Archaeology in the Biblical World* 2.2 (1994): 8–21.

———. "Israel's Forty Years in the Wilderness: A Geographic and Socio-spatial Analysis." In *Lexham Geographic Commentary on the Pentateuch.* Edited by Barry J. Beitzel. Bellingham, WA: Lexham Press, forthcoming.

———. "The *Via Maris* in Literary and Cartographic Sources." *BA* 54.2 (1991): 64–75.

Bekker-Nielsen, Tønnes. *The Roads of Ancient Cyprus.* Copenhagen: Museum Tusculanum Press, 2004.

Berggren, J. Lennart, and Alexander Jones. *Ptolemy's Geography: An Annotated Translation of the Theoretical Chapters.* Princeton: Princeton University Press, 2000.

Bietak, Manfred. "Comments on the Exodus." Pages 163–71 in *Egypt, Israel, Sinai: Archaeological and Historical Relationships in the Biblical Period.* Edited by Anson F. Rainey. Tel Aviv: Tel Aviv University, 1987.

———. "On the Historicity of the Exodus: What Egyptology Today Can Contribute to Assessing the Biblical Account of the Sojourn in Egypt." Pages 17–37 in *Israel's Exodus in Transdisciplinary Perspective: Text, Archaeology, Culture, and Geoscience.* Edited by Thomas E. Levy, Thomas Schneider, and William H. C. Propp. New York: Springer, 2015.

Blue, Lucy. "Locating the Harbour: Myos Hormos/Quseir
    al-Qadim; a Roman and Islamic Port on the Red Sea Coast
    of Egypt." *IJNA* 36 (2007): 265–81.

Blum, Howard *The Gold of Exodus: The Discovery of the True Mount
    Sinai.* New York: Simon & Schuster, 1998.

Bochart, Samuel. *Geographia Sacra, seu Phaleg et Canaan.* Leiden:
    Boutesteyn & Luchtmans, 1692.

Borstad, Karen A. "History from Geography: The Initial Route of
    the *Via Nova Traiana* in Jordan." *Levant* 40 (2008): 55–70.

Brotzman, Ellis, and Raymond Martin. *Jonah: Computer Generated
    Tools for the Correlated Greek and Hebrew Texts.* Computer
    Bible 59A. Wooster, OH: Biblical Research Associates, 1998.

Bruckner, James. *Jonah, Nahum, Habakkuk, Zephaniah.* NIVAC.
    Grand Rapids: Zondervan, 2004.

Brugsch, Heinrich Karl. *Hieroglyphisch-Demotisches Wörterbuch.* 7
    vols. Leipzig: Hinrichs, 1867–1882.

Budd, Philip J. *Numbers.* WBC 5. Waco, TX: Word, 1984.

Bunbury, E. H. *A History of Ancient Geography: Among the Greeks
    and Romans from the Earliest Ages Till the Fall of the Roman
    Empire.* 2 vols. New York: Dover, 1959.

Burstein, Stanley J. *Agatharchides of Cnidus on the Erythraean Sea.*
    London: Hakluyt Society, 1989.

Burton, Richard F. "Itineraries of the Second Khedivial Expedition:
    Memoir Explaining the New Map of Midian Made by the
    Egyptian Staff-Officers." *Journal of the Royal Geographical
    Society of London* 49 (1879): 1–150.

Butler, Howard Crosby. "Desert Syria, the Land of a Lost
    Civilization." *Geographical Review* 9.2 (1920): 77–108.

———. "Trajan's Road from Boṣra to the Red Sea: The Section
    between Boṣra and 'Ammân." Pages vii–xvi in *Publications
    of the Princeton University Archaeological Expeditions to
    Syria in 1904–05 and 1909; Vol. 4, Division 3, Greek and
    Latin Inscriptions in Syria; Section A, Southern Syria, Part
    2: Southern Haurân, Appendix.* Edited by Enno Littmann,

David Magie Jr., and Duane Reed Stuart. 7 vols. Leiden: Brill, 1910.

Calvin, John. *Ioannis Calvini opera quae supersunt omnia*. Vol. 23. Corpus Reformatorum vol. 51. Edited by William Baum, Edward Cunitz, and Edward Reuss. Brunsvigae: Schwetschke, 1882.

Caminos, Ricardo A. *Late-Egyptian Miscellanies*. London: Oxford University Press, 1954.

Caner, Daniel F. *History and Hagiography from the Late Antique Sinai*. Liverpool: Liverpool University Press, 2010.

Casson, Lionel. *The Periplus Maris Erythraei: Text with Introduction, Translation, and Commentary*. Princeton: Princeton University Press, 1989.

Cassuto, Umberto. *A Commentary on the Book of Exodus*. Jerusalem: Magnes, 1967.

Childs, Brevard S. *The Book of Exodus: A Critical, Theological Commentary*. OTL. Philadelphia: Westminster, 1974.

Christensen, Duane L. *Deuteronomy 1:1–21:9*. WBC. Nashville: Nelson, 2001.

Clements, R. E. *Exodus*. CBC. Cambridge: Cambridge University Press, 1972.

Cohen, Getzel M. *The Hellenistic Settlements in Syria, the Red Sea Basin, and North Africa*. Berkeley: University of California Press, 2016.

Cole, R. Dennis. *Numbers*. NAC. Nashville: Broadman & Holman, 2000.

Craigie, Peter C. *The Book of Deuteronomy*. NICOT. Grand Rapids: Eerdman, 1976.

Dahari, Uzi. *Monastic Settlements in South Sinai in the Byzantine Period: The Archaeological Remains*. IAAR 9. Jerusalem: Israel Antiquities Authority, 2000.

Davies, Graham I. *The Way of the Wilderness: A Geographical Study of the Wilderness Itineraries in the Old Testament*. Cambridge: Cambridge University Press, 1979.

Dayan, Galit. "The Term *p3-ṯwf*'in the Spiegelberg Papyrus." Pages 133–35 in *Jerusalem Studies in Egyptology*. Edited by Irene Shirun-Grumach. ÄAT 40. Wiesbaden: Harrassowitz, 1998.

Delitzsch, Franz. *A New Commentary on Genesis*. Edinburgh: T&T Clark, 1899.

Dever, William G. "Is There Any Archaeological Evidence for the Exodus?" Pages 67–86 in *Exodus: The Egyptian Evidence*. Edited by Ernest S. Frerichs and Leonard H. Lesko. Winona Lake, IN: Eisenbrauns, 1997.

DeVries, LaMoine F. "Jeshimon." *ABD* 3:769.

Di Berardino, Angelo, ed. *Historical Atlas of Ancient Christianity*. St. Davids, PA: ICCS Press, 2013.

Dilke, O. A. W. "The Culmination of Greek Cartography in Ptolemy." With additional material supplied by the editors. Pages 177–200 in *Cartography in Prehistoric, Ancient, and Medieval Europe and the Mediterranean*. Edited by J. B. Harley and David Woodward. Vol. 1 of *The History of Cartography*. Edited by J. B. Harley and David Woodward. Chicago: University of Chicago Press, 1987.

———. *Greek and Roman Maps*. Ithaca, NY: Cornell University Press, 1985.

Diller, Aubrey. Review of *Claudius Ptolemy: The Geography*, by Edward Stevenson. *Isis* 22 (1935): 535–39.

Dittenberger, Wilhelm. *Orientis Graeci: Inscriptiones Selectae*. 2 vols. Leipzig: Hirzel, 1903–1905.

Donner, Herbert. *The Mosaic Map of Madaba: An Introductory Guide*. Kampen: Kok Pharos, 1992.

Dozeman, Thomas B. "Biblical Geography and Critical Spatial Studies." Pages 87–108 in *Constructions in Space I: Theory, Geography, and Narrative*. Edited by Jon L. Berquist and Claudia V. Camp. LHBOTS 481. London: T&T Clark, 2007.

———. *Commentary on Exodus*. Grand Rapids: Eerdmans, 2009.

Driver, S. R. *The Book of Genesis*. London: Methuen, 1911.

———. *A Critical and Exegetical Commentary on Deuteronomy.* 3rd ed. ICC. Edinburgh: T&T Clark, 1965.

———. *Notes on the Hebrew Text and the Topography of the Books of Samuel.* 2nd ed. Oxford: Clarendon, 1913.

Englisch, Brigitte. *Ordo orbis terrae: Die Weltsicht in den Mappae mundi des frühen und hohen Mittelalters.* Berlin: Akademie, 2002.

Enns, Peter. "Exodus Route and Wilderness Itinerary." *DOTP,* 272–80.

Erman, Adolf, and Hermann Grapow. *Wörterbuch der ägyptischen Sprache.* 7 vols. Berlin: Akademie, 1926–1931. Repr., 1982.

Fischer, David Hackett. *Historical Fallacies: Toward a Logic of Historical Thought.* New York: HarperPerennial, 1970.

Fritz, Glen A. "The Lost Sea of the Exodus: A Modern Geographical Analysis." PhD diss., Texas State University, 2006.

———. *The Lost Sea of the Exodus: A Modern Geographical Analysis.* San Antonio, TX: GeoTech, 2016.

Gardiner, Alan H. *Late-Egyptian Miscellanies.* Brussels: Édition de la Fondation égyptologique Reine Élisabeth, 1937.

Garrett, Duane A. *A Commentary on Exodus.* Kregel Exegetical Library. Grand Rapids: Kregel Academic, 2014.

Germer-Durand, R. "Exploration épigraphique de Gerasa." *RB* 4 (1895): 374–400.

———. "Rapport sur l'exploration archéologique en 1903 de la voie Romaine entre Ammân et Bostra (Arabie)." *Bulletin archéologique du Comité des travaux historiques et scientifiques* 11 (1904): 3–43.

Gesenius, Wilhelm. *Gesenius' Hebrew and Chaldee Lexicon to the Old Testament Scripture.* Grand Rapids: Baker, 1979.

Geyer, Paul. "Theodosii, De situ Terrae Sanctae." Pages 113–25 in *Itineraria et alia geographica.* Edited by Ezio Franceschini, Robert Weber, and Paul Geyer. CCSL 175. Turnhout: Brepols, 1965.

Gharaibeh, Ahmed Abdulla. "Heat Source Study and Geothermal
    Reservoir Assessment for the Zarqa Ma'in—Dab'a Area,
    Central Jordan." *United Nations University, Reports* 17 (2008):
    221–46.
Goedicke, Hans G. "Tjeku." *LÄ* 6 col. 609.
Gordon, Robert. *1 & 2 Samuel*. Exeter: Paternoster, 1986.
Görg, Manfred. "Etam und Pitom." *BN* 51 (1980): 9–10.
Graf, David F. "Map 76 Sinai." *BAGRW* 2:1140–46.
———. "The Origin of the Nabataeans." *Aram* 2 (1990): 45–75.
———. "Roman Roads East of the Jordan." Pages 230–34 in *The
    Madaba Map Centenary 1897–1997: Travelling Through the
    Byzantine Umayyad Period*. Edited by Michele Piccirillo and
    Eugenio Alliata. Jerusalem: Studium Biblicum Franciscanum,
    1999.
———. *Rome and the Arabian Frontier: From the Nabataeans to the
    Saracens*. Brookfield, VT: Ashgate, 1997.
———. "The *Via Militaris* in Arabia." *DOP* 51 (1997): 271–81.
———. "The *Via Nova Traiana* in Arabia Petraea." Pages 241–67 in
    *The Roman and Byzantine East: Some Recent Archaeological
    Research*. Edited by John H. Humphrey. JRASup 14. Ann
    Arbor: Journal of Roman Archaeology, 1995.
Gray, John. *A Critical and Exegetical Commentary on Numbers*. ICC.
    Edinburgh: T&T Clark, 1976.
Groll, Sarah I. "The Egyptian Background of the Exodus and
    the Crossing of the Reed Sea: A New Reading of Papyrus
    Anastasi VIII." Pages 173–92 in *Jerusalem Studies in
    Egyptology*. Edited by Irene Shirun-Grumach. ÄAT 40.
    Wiesbaden: Harrassowitz, 1998.
Gysens, Jacqueline Calzini. "Interim Report on the Rabbathmoab
    and Qaṣr Rabbah Project." *East and West* 58 (2008): 53–86.
Hamilton, Victor. *The Book of Genesis: Chapters 18–50*. NICOT.
    Grand Rapids: Eerdmans, 1995.
Harley, J. B., and David Woodward, eds. *The History of
    Cartography: Cartography in Prehistoric, Ancient and Medieval*

Europe and the Mediterranean. 6 vols. Chicago: University of Chicago Press, 1987–2015. https://www.press.uchicago.edu/books/HOC/index.html.

Harrison, R. K. *Numbers: An Exegetical Commentary*. Grand Rapids: Baker, 1992.

Harvey, P. D. A. *The History of Topographical Maps: Symbols, Pictures, and Surveys*. London: Thames & Hudson, 1980.

Hess, Richard S. "Onomastics of the Exodus Generation in the Book of Exodus." Pages 37–48 in *"Did I Not Bring Israel Out of Egypt?": Biblical, Archaeological, and Egyptological Perspectives on the Exodus Narratives*. Edited by James K. Hoffmeier, Alan R. Millard, and Gary A. Rendsburg. BBRSup 13. Winona Lake, IN: Eisenbrauns, 2016.

Hoch, James E. *Semitic Words In Egyptian Texts of the New Kingdom and Third Intermediate Period*. Princeton: Princeton University Press, 1994.

Hoffmeier, James K. *Israel in Egypt: The Evidence for the Authenticity of the Exodus Tradition*. New York: Oxford University Press, 1996.

Hoffmeier, James K., Alan R. Millard, and Gary A. Rendsburg, eds. *"Did I Not Bring Israel Out of Egypt?: Biblical, Archaeological, and Egyptological Perspectives on the Exodus Narratives*. BBRSup 13. Winona Lake, IN: Eisenbrauns, 2016.

Holladay, John S. *Cities of the Delta, Part III, Tell el-Maskhuṭa: Preliminary Report on the Wadi Tumilat Project 1978–1979*. ARCER 6. Malibu, CA: Undena, 1982.

Hool, Alexander. *Searching for Sinai: The Location of Revelation*. Nanuet, NY: Feldheim, 2017.

Humphreys, Colin J. *The Miracles of Exodus: A Scientist's Discovery of the Extraordinary Natural Causes of the Biblical Stories*. San Francisco: Harper, 2003.

Jacob, Irene, and Walter Jacob. "Flora." *ABD* 2:803–817.

Jaussen, A. "Voyage du Sinai." *RB* 12 (1903): 100–111.

Jones, Alexander. "Ptolemy's Geography: Mapmaking and the Scientific Enterprise." Pages 109–28 in *Ancient Perspectives: Maps and Their Place in Mesopotamia, Egypt, Greece and Rome*. Edited by Richard J. A. Talbert. Chicago: University of Chicago Press, 2012.

Kent, Roland G. *Old Persian: Grammar, Texts, Lexicon*. 2nd ed. American Oriental Series 33. New Haven: American Oriental Society, 1953.

Kerkeslager, Allen. "Jewish Pilgrimage and Jewish Identity in Hellenistic and Early Roman Egypt." Pages 99–225 in *Pilgrimage and Holy Space in Late Antique Egypt*. Edited by David Frankfurter. RGRW 134. Leiden: Brill, 1998.

———. "Mt. Sinai—in Arabia? Ancient Jewish Tradition Locates Holy Mountain." Pages 33–46 in *Mysteries of the Bible: From the Location of Eden to the Shroud of Turin; a Collection of Essays Published by the Biblical Archaeology Society*. Edited by Molly Dewsnap Meinhardt. Washington, DC: Biblical Archaeology Society, 2004.

Khouri, Rami G., and Donald Whitcomb. *Aqaba: "Port of Palestine on the China Sea."* Amman: Al Kutba, 1988.

Kitchen, Kenneth A. *Ancient Orient and Old Testament*. Downers Grove, IL: InterVarsity Press, 1966.

———. "From the Brickfields of Egypt." *TynBul* 27 (1976): 137–47.

———. "Egyptians and Hebrews, from Raʿamses to Jericho." Pages 65–131 in *The Origin of Early Israel—Current Debate: Biblical, Historical and Archaeological Perspectives*. Edited by Shmuel Aḥituv and Eliezer D. Oren. Beer-Sheva 12. Beer-Sheva: Ben-Gurion University of the Negev Press, 1998.

———. *On the Reliability of the Old Testament*. Grand Rapids: Eerdmans, 2003.

Klein, Ralph. W. *1 Samuel*. 2nd ed. WBC 10. Nashville: Nelson, 2008.

Kohlenberger, John R., III. *Jonah and Nahum*. Chicago: Moody Press, 1984.

Lambdin, Thomas O. "Egyptian Loan Words in the Old Testament." *JAOS* 73 (1953): 145–55.

Latourette, Kenneth Scott. *A History of Christianity*. New York: Harper & Row, 1953.

Laurence, Ray. *The Roads of Roman Italy: Mobility and Cultural Change*. London: Routledge, 1999.

Lecoq, Pierre. *Les inscriptions de la Perse achéménide*. Paris: Gallimard, 1997.

Leprohon, Ronald J. *The Great Name: Ancient Egyptian Royal Titulary*. WAW 33. Atlanta: Society of Biblical Literature, 2013.

Levine, Baruch A. *Numbers 1–20: A New Translation with Introduction and Commentary*. AB 4. New York: Doubleday, 1993.

———. *Numbers 21–36: A New Translation with Introduction and Commentary*. AB 4A. New York: Doubleday, 2000.

Levy, Thomas E., Thomas Schneider, and William H. C. Propp, eds. *Israel's Exodus in Transdisciplinary Perspective: Text, Archaeology, Culture, and Geoscience*. New York: Springer, 2013.

Lewin, Ariel S. "Rome's Relations with the Arab/Indigenous People in the First–Third Centuries." Pages 113–43 in *Inside and Out: Interactions between Rome and the Peoples on the Arabian and Egyptian Frontiers in Late Antiquity*. Edited by Jitse H. K. Dijkstra and Greg Fisher. Late Antique History and Religion 8. Leuven: Peeters, 2014.

Limburg, James. *Jonah: A Commentary*. OTL. Louisville: Westminster John Knox, 1993.

Lindberg, David C. "Science and the Early Christian Church." *Isis* 74 (1983): 509–30.

Lindberg, David C., and Ronald L. Numbers, eds. *When Science and Christianity Meet*. Chicago: University of Chicago Press, 2003.

MacAdam, Henry Innes. *Studies in the History of the Roman Province of Arabia: The Northern Sector*. BARIS 295. Oxford: BAR, 1986.

MacDonald, Burton, Gary O. Rollefson, and Duane W. Roller. "The Wadi el Hasa Survey 1981: A Preliminary Report." *ADAJ* 26 (1982): 117–31, pls. 27–34.

Magie, David, Jr. "Milestones Found on Trajan's Road between Boṣra and 'Ammân." Pages xvii–xxviii in *Publications of the Princeton University Archaeological Expeditions to Syria in 1904-1905 and 1909; Vol. 4, Division 3, Greek and Latin Inscriptions in Syria; Section A, Southern Syria, Part 2: Southern Haurân, Appendix*. Edited by Enno Littmann, David Magie Jr., and Duane Reed Stuart. 7 vols. Leiden: Brill, 1910.

Marchadour, Alain, and David Neuhaus. *The Land, the Bible, and History: Toward the Land That I Will Show You*. New York: Fordham University Press, 2007.

Mason. Kenneth, ed. *Western Arabia and the Red Sea*. Geographical Handbook Series, BR 527. Oxford: Naval Intelligence Division, 1946.

Mathews, Kenneth. *Genesis 11:27–50:26*. NAC 1B. Nashville: Broadman & Holman, 2005.

Mayes, A. D. H. *Deuteronomy*. NCB. Grand Rapids: Eerdmans, 1981.

Mayor, Adrienne. "Scorpions in Antiquity." *Wonders and Marvels*. http://www.wondersandmarvels.com/2013/12/scorpions-in-antiquity.html.

McCarter, P. Kyle. *1 Samuel: A New Translation with Introduction, Notes and Commentary*. AB 8. New York: Doubleday, 1980.

Meineke, Augusti. *Stephan von Byzanz: Ethnika*. Graz: Akademische Drucke & Verlagsanstalt, 1958.

Merrill, Eugene H. *Deuteronomy*. NAC 4. Nashville: Broadman & Holman, 1994.

Milgrom, Jacob. *Numbers: The Traditional Hebrew Text with the New JPS Translation*. JPS Torah Commentary. Philadelphia: Jewish Publication Society, 1990.

Mittmann, Siegfried. *Beiträge zur Siedlungs- und Territorialgeschichte des nördlichen Ostjordanlandes*. ADPV. Wiesbaden: Harrassowitz, 1970.

Moritz, Bernhard. *Der Sinaikult in heidnischer Zeit*. Abhandlungen der königlichen Gesellschaft der Wissenschaften zu Göttingen, neue folge 16/2. Berlin: Weidmann, 1916.

Morris, Ellen Fowles. *The Architecture of Imperialism: Military Bases and the Evolution of Foreign Policy in Egypt's New Kingdom*. PAe 22. Leiden: Brill, 2005.

Muchiki, Yoshiyuki. *Egyptian Proper Names and Loanwords in North-West Semitic*. SBLDS 173. Atlanta: Society of Biblical Literature, 1999.

Müller, Carolus. *Geographi Graeci Minores*. 2 vols. Paris: Didot, 1861.

Müller, F. Max. "A Contribution to the Exodus Geography." *PSBA* 10 (1888): 467–77.

Musil, Alois. *Arabia Petraea*. 3 vols. Kaiserliche Akademie der Wissenschaften. Vienna: Hölder, 1907–1908.

———. *The Northern Ḥeǧâz: A Topographical Itinerary*. Oriental Explorations and Studies 1. New York: AMS Press, 1926.

Nau, F. "Le texte grec des récits du moine Anastase sur les saints pères du Sinaï." *OC* 2 (1902): 58–89.

Nebenzahl, Kenneth. *Maps of the Holy Land: Images of Terra Sancta through Two Millennia*. New York: Abbeville Press, 1986.

Negev, Abraham. "The Nabateans and the Provincia Arabia." *ANRW* 2.8.520–686.

Nixey, Catherine. *The Darkening Age: The Christian Destruction of the Classical World*. Boston: Houghton Mifflin Harcourt, 2018.

Nobbe, Carolus Fredericus Augustus. *Claudii Ptolemaei Geographia*. 3 vols. Leipzig: Tauchnitus, 1843–1845.

Noonan, Benjamin J. "Egyptian Loanwords as Evidence for the Authenticity of the Exodus and Wilderness Traditions." Pages 49–67 in *"Did I Not Bring Israel Out of Egypt?": Biblical, Archaeological, and Egyptological Perspectives on the Exodus Narratives*. Edited by James K. Hoffmeier, Alan R. Millard, and Gary A. Rendsburg. BBRSup 13. Winona Lake, IN: Eisenbrauns, 2016.

Noth, Martin. "Der Schauplatz des Meereswunders." Pages 181–90 in *Festschrift Otto Eissfeldt zum 60. Geburtstage 1. September 1947: Dargebracht von Freunden und Verehrern*. Edited by Johann Fück. Halle: Niemeyer, 1947.

———. *Numbers: A Commentary*. OTL. London: SCM, 1968.

Notley, R. Steven, and Ze'ev Safrai. *Eusebius, Onomasticon: The Place Names of Divine Scripture*. Leiden: Brill, 2005.

Oblath, Michael D. *The Exodus Itinerary Sites: Their Locations from the Perspective of the Biblical Sources*. StBibLit 55. New York: Lang, 2004.

O'Connor, Michael. "The Etymology of *Saracen* in Aramaic and Pre-Islamic Arabic Contexts." Pages 603–32 in *The Defence of the Roman and Byzantine East: Proceedings of a Colloquium Held at the University of Sheffield in April 1986*. Edited by Philip Freeman and David Kennedy. 2 vols. British Institute of Archaeology at Ankara Monograph 8. BARIS 297. Oxford: BAR, 1986.

Omran, Mohamed A. A., and Alistar McVean. "Intraspecific Variation in Scorpion *LEIURUS QUINQUESTRIATUS* Venom Collected from Egypt (Sinai and Aswan Deserts)." *Journal of Toxicology: Toxin Reviews* 19 (2000): 247–64.

Ortelius, Abraham. *Theatrum orbis terrarum*. Antwerp: van Diest, 1570.

Parker, S. Thomas. "Projecting Power on the Periphery: Rome's Arabian Frontier East of the Dead Sea." Pages 349–57 in *Crossing Jordan: North American Contributions to the Archaeology of Jordan*. Edited by Thomas E. Levy, P. M.

Michele Daviau, Randall W. Younker, and May Shaer.
London: Equinox, 2007.

———. "The Roman ʿAqaba Project: the 1994 Campaign." *ADAJ* 40 (1996): 231–57.

———. "The Roman Port of Aila: Economic Connections with the Red Sea Littoral." Pages 79–84 in *Connected Hinterlands: Proceedings of Red Sea Project IV Held at the University of Southampton, September 2008.* Edited by Lucy Blue, John Cooper, Ross Thomas, and Julian Whitewright. Society for Arabian Studies Monographs 8. BARIS 2052. Oxford: Archaeopress, 2009.

Parr, P. J., G. L. Harding, and J. E. Dayton. "Preliminary Survey in N. W. Arabia, 1968." *Bulletin of the Institute of Archaeology, University of London* 10 (1971): 23–61.

Pekáry, Thomas. *Untersuchungen zu den römischen Reichsstrassen.* Antiquitas. Abhandlungen zur alten Geschichte 17. Bonn: Habelt, 1968.

Plaut, W. Gunther. *The Torah, A Modern Commentary: Numbers.* New York: Union of American Hebrew Congregations, 1979.

Preaux, Claire. "Une source nouvelle sur l'annexion de l'Arabie par Trajan: Les papyrus de Michigan 465 et 466." *Phoibos* 5 (1950–1951): 1–2:123–39.

Prewett, J. F. "Jeshimon." *ISBE* 2:1032–33.

Propp, William H. C. *Exodus 19–40: A New Translation with Introduction and Commentary.* AB 2A. New York: Doubleday, 2006.

Rainey, Anson F. "Toponymic Problems (cont.)." *TA* 9 (1982): 130–36.

Rainey, Anson F., and R. Steven Notley. *The Sacred Bridge.* Jerusalem: Carta, 2006.

Raschke, M. "New Studies in Roman Commerce with the East." *ANRW* 2.9.2:604–1361.

Ray, Himanshu Prabha. *The Archaeology of Seafaring in Ancient South Asia*. Cambridge World Archaeology. Cambridge: Cambridge University Press, 2003.

Redford, Donald B. "Pithom." *LÄ* 4:1054–58.

Roll, Israel. "The Roads in Roman-Byzantine Palaestina and Arabia." Pages 109–13 in *The Madaba Map Centenary, 1897–1997; Travelling Through the Byzantine Umayyad Period*. Edited by Michele Piccirillo and Eugenio Alliata. Jerusalem: Studium Biblicum Franciscanum, 1999.

Roller, Duane W. *Eratosthenes' Geography: Fragments Collected and Translated with Commentary and Additional Material*. Princeton: Princeton University Press, 2010.

Roskop, Angela R. *The Wilderness Itineraries: Genre, Geography, and the Growth of Torah*. HACL 3. Winona Lake, IN: Eisenbrauns, 2011.

Rostovtzeff, M. *The Social and Economic History of the Roman Empire*. 2nd ed. 2 vols. Oxford: Clarendon, 1998.

Rubin, Aaron D. "Egyptian Loanwords." *EHLL* 1:793–94.

Ruppel, M. Walter. *Les Temples Immergés de la Nubie, Der Tempel von Dakke*. 3 vols. Cairo: Institut français d'archéologie orientale, 1930.

Sarna, Nahum M. *Exodus: The Traditional Hebrew Text with the New JPS Translation*. JPS Torah Commentary. Philadelphia: Jewish Publication Society, 1991.

Sartre, Maurice. "Nouvelles Inscriptions Grecques et Latines de Bostra." *AAAS* 22 (1972): 167–91.

Sasson, Jack M. *Jonah: A New Translation with Introduction, Commentary, and Interpretation*. AB 24B. New York: Doubleday, 1990.

Schmidt, Mauricius. *Hesychii Alexandrini lexicon*. Jenae: Maukiana, 1864.

Seely, David R. "Shur, Wilderness of." *ABD* 5:1230.

Seely, Jo Ann H. "Succoth." *ABD* 6:217–18.

Sidebotham, Steven. *Berenike and the Ancient Maritime Spice Route.* Berkeley: University of California Press, 2011.

———. "Red Sea Trade." *ABD* 5:642–44.

Silberman, Alain. *Pomponius Mela, Chorographie.* Collection des Universités de France. Paris: Belles Lettres, 1988.

Simons, J. J. *The Geographical and Topographical Texts of the Old Testament.* Leiden: Brill, 1959.

Speidel, Michael Alexander. "The Roman Army in Arabia." *ANRW* 2.8:687–730.

Speiser, E. A. *Genesis.* AB 1. New York: Doubleday, 1964.

Staccioli, Romolo Augusto. *The Roads of the Romans.* Los Angeles: Getty Museum, 2003.

Stahl, William Harris. *Ptolemy's Geography: A Select Bibliography.* New York: New York Public Library, 1953.

Stevenson, Edward I. *Claudius Ptolemy: The Geography, Based upon Greek and Latin Manuscripts and Important Late Fifteenth and Early Sixteenth Century Printed Editions.* New York: New York Public Library, 1932.

Strong, James. *Strong's Exhaustive Concordance.* Nashville: Nelson, 1990.

Stuart, Douglas. *Hosea–Jonah.* WBC 31. Waco, TX: Word, 1987.

Stückelberger, Alfred, and Gerd Grasshoff. *Klaudios Ptolemaios: Handbuch der Geographie, Griechisch-Deutsch.* 2 vols. Basel: Schwabe, 2006.

Tarn, W. W. "Ptolemy II and Arabia." *JEA* 15 (1929): 9–25.

Taylor, Joan E., and Shimon Gibson. "Qumran Connected: The Qumran Pass and Paths of the North-Western Dead Sea." Pages 163–208 in *Qumran und die Archäologie: Texte und Kontexte.* Edited by Jörg Frey, Carsten Claussen, and Nadine Kessler. WUNT 278. Tübingen: Mohr Siebeck, 2011.

Thayer, William. "Ptolemy: The Geography." http://penelope. uchicago.edu/Thayer/E/Gazetteer/Periods/Roman/_Texts/ Ptolemy/home.html.

———. "The Road Is Gone and as Often, Only the Milestone Remains." http://penelope.uchicago.edu/Thayer/E/ Gazetteer/Places/Europe/Italy. 2012.

Thomas, Ross I. "Port Communities and the Erythraean Sea Trade." *British Museum Studies in Ancient Egypt and Sudan* 18 (2012): 169–99.

Thomsen, P. "Die römischen Meilensteine der Provinzen Syria, Arabia und Palaestina." *ZDPV* 40 (1917): 1–103.

Thomson, J. Oliver. *History of Ancient Geography*. New York: Biblo & Tannen, 1965.

Toomer, G. J. "Ptolemy." *Complete Dictionary of Scientific Biography*. Detroit: Cengage, 2008. https://www.encyclopedia.com/ people/science-and-technology/astronomy-biographies/ ptolemy.

Tscherikower, Victor. *Die hellenistischen Städtegründungen von Alexander dem Grossen bis auf die Römerzeit*. Philologus Supplement 19. New York: Arno 1973.

Tsumura, David. *The First Book of Samuel*. NICOT. Grand Rapids: Eerdmans, 2007.

Tuplin, Christopher. "Darius' Suez Canal and Persian Imperialism." Pages 237–83 in *Asia Minor and Egypt: Old Cultures in a New Empire; Proceedings of the 1988 Groningen Achaemenid History Workshop*. Edited by H. Sancisi-Weerdenburg and Amélie Kuhrt. Achaemenid History 6. Leiden: Nederlands Instituut voor het Nabije Oosten, 1991.

Van Dijk, Jacobus. "The Amarna Period and the Later New Kingdom (c. 1352–1069 BC)." Pages 265–307 in *The Oxford History of Ancient Egypt*. Edited by Ian Shaw. New York: Oxford University Press, 2003.

Van Rengen, Wilfried. "The Written Material from the Graeco-Roman Period." Pages 335–38 in *Myos Hormos—Quseir al-Qadim: Roman and Islamic Ports on the Red Sea 2; Finds from the Excavations 1999–2003*. Edited by David Peacock

and Lucy Blue. University of Southampton Series in
Archaeology 6. BARIS 2286. Oxford: Archaeopress, 2011.

Virga, Vincent. *Cartographia: Mapping Civilizations*. New York:
Little, Brown, 2008.

Walker, Peter. "Pilgrimage in the Early Church." Pages 73–91 in
Explorations in a Christian Theology of Pilgrimage. Edited
by Craig Bartholomew and Fred Hughes. Burlington, VT:
Ashgate, 2004.

Walton, John H. *Jonah*. Bible Study Commentary. Grand Rapids:
Zondervan, 1982.

Ward, William A. "The Semitic Biconsonantal Root *SP* and the
Common Origin of Egyptian *ČWF* and Hebrew *SÛP*:
'Marsh(-Plant).'" *VT* 24 (1974): 339–49.

Weinfeld, Moshe. *Deuteronomy 1–11: A New Translation with
Introduction and Commentary*. AB 5. New York: Doubleday,
1991.

Wenham, Gordon J. *Genesis 16–50*. WBC 2. Dallas: Word, 1994.

———. *Numbers*. TOTC. Downers Grove, IL: InterVarsity Press,
1981.

Westermann, Claus. *Genesis 12–36*. CC. Minneapolis: Fortress, 1995.

Wevers, John William. *Notes on the Greek Text of Numbers*. SCS 46.
Atlanta: Scholars Press, 1998.

Whitcomb, Donald. "Islamic Archaeology." *The Oriental Institute
2002–2003 Annual Report*. Chicago: Oriental Institute of the
University of Chicago, 2003. https://oi.uchicago.edu/sites/
oi.uchicago.edu/files/uploads/shared/docs/ar/01-10/02-
03/02-03_Islamic_Arch.pdf.

Whitfield, Peter. *The Image of the World: 20 Centuries of World Maps*.
London: British Library, 1994.

Wilkinson, John. "Christian Pilgrims in Jerusalem during the
Byzantine Period." *PEQ* 108 (1976): 75–101.

———. *Egeria's Travels to the Holy Land*. 3rd ed. Warminster: Aris &
Phillips, 1999.

————. *Jerusalem Pilgrims before the Crusades*. Warminster: Aris & Phillips, 1977. 2nd ed., 2002.

————. "Jewish Holy Places and the Origins of Christian Pilgrimage." Pages 41–53 in *The Blessings of Pilgrimage*. Edited by Robert G. Ousterhout. Urbana: University of Illinois Press, 1990.

Wolff, Hans Walter. *Obadiah and Jonah: A Commentary*. Translated by Margaret Kohl. CC. Minneapolis: Augsburg, 1987.

Zlotowitz, Meir. *Jonah: A New Translation with a Commentary Anthologized from Talmudic, Midrashic, and Rabbinic Sources*. ArtScroll Tanach. Brooklyn: Mesorah, 1978.

GENERAL INDEX

SCRIPTURE INDEX

Old Testament

New Testament

ANCIENT SOURCES INDEX

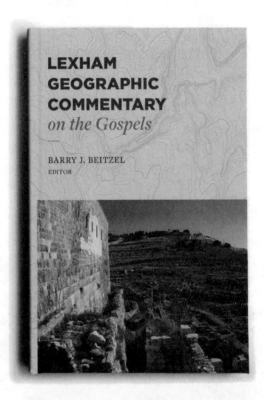